D1195658

SEPTEMBER MOURN
The Dunker Church of Antietam Battlefield

Alann Schmidt and Terry Barkley

Savas Beatie
California

Library of Congress Cataloging-in-Publication Data

Names: Schmidt, Alann. | Barkley, Terry, author.
Title: September mourn : the Dunker Church of Antietam Battlefield /
by Alann Schmidt and Terry Barkley.
Description: First edition. | El Dorado Hills : Savas Beatie, 2018. |
Includes bibliographical references and index.
Identifiers: LCCN 2018008397| ISBN 9781611214017 (hardcover: alk. paper) |
ISBN 9781611214499 (pbk: alk. Paper) | ISBN 9781611214024 (ebk)
Subjects: LCSH: Dunker Church (Antietam National Battlefield) | Sharpsburg
(Md.)—Church history.
Classification: LCC BX7831.A68 S36 2018 | DDC 286/.5—dc23
LC record available at https://lccn.loc.gov/2018008397

First Edition, First Printing

SB

Savas Beatie LLC
989 Governor Drive, Suite 102
El Dorado Hills, CA 95762
Phone: 916-941-6896
(web) www.savasbeatie.com
(E-mail) sales@savasbeatie.com

Our titles are available at special discounts for bulk purchases. For more details, contact us us at sales@savasbeatie.com.

Proudly printed in the United States of America.

Alann Schmidt

To Rev. John Schildt for his prolific dedication in promoting Antietam's local history, and for being such a kind, generous, and humble example. Up to this point, his *Drums Along the Antietam* was the only major work in print to cover the specific significance of the Dunker Church to the Antietam story. I hope this book takes it to the next level and makes you proud. Please know that in the "evening dews and damps" you have made a wonderful impact.

Terry Barkley

In memory of Rev. H. Austin Cooper, Church of the Brethren minister and historian, and one at the forefront of getting the Dunker Church reconstructed on the Antietam battlefield; and for my paternal great-grandfather, Pvt. William D. Barkley, Company D, 31st Georgia, who was severely wounded at Antietam within sight of the Dunker Church, September 17, 1862.

September Mourn

The Dunker Church of Antietam

Alann D. Schmidt and Terry W. Barkley

Foreword by Ted Alexander
Chief Historian, Antietam National Battlefield (Ret.)

Table of Contents

Table of Contents (continued)

List of Maps

List of Images

Photos and illustrations have been inserted throughout the book
for the convenience of the reader.

Foreword

In 1745, Daniel Dulaney of Maryland wrote to Governor Samuel Ogle, "You would be surprised how much the country is improved beyond the mountains, especially by the Germans, who are the best people that can be to settle a wilderness." These settlers, often referred to as "Pennsylvania Germans" because of their place of origin in the "New World," would become the major group to settle Western Maryland. The majority of these pioneers were Lutheran or Reformed. However, a visible and notable minority were "Dunkers" or German Baptist Brethren.

The land the "Dunkers" settled was a virtual wild frontier in the mid-eighteenth century. Moving across the South Mountain range, they settled along Antietam Creek, named after a Delaware Indian word meaning "swift flowing water." Their farms were in the "Great Valley" running from Canada all the way south to Alabama. In this particular region in Maryland, it was known as the Cumberland Valley, the Antietam Valley, or the Hagerstown Valley.

The soil in this area has a bedrock that is mainly limestone. Limestone outcroppings form the rocky slopes of pastures. This provided a challenge to the farmers who tilled the soil, but the challenge was not insurmountable. The industrious Germans, including the Dunkers, turned the abundance of stone to their advantage, using it to construct stone wall fencing, barns, and farm houses. The invading Confederate soldiers in 1862 marveled at this sturdy architecture. But it was the small white-washed brick church, built in 1853 along the Hagerstown/Sharpsburg Pike, that would become far more famous than any other structure in the region.

The Dunker Church remains among three iconic churches in American military history. The first is the Alamo, widely considered a shrine by

Texans, other Americans, and even many people around the world. There, about 200 men fought to the death in a sacrifice that has been honored in books, magazines, movies, and television. The next iconic church is the humble log structure of Shiloh Church in Tennessee. Fought on April 6-7, 1862, Shiloh was the first big bloodbath in the Civil War. The little country church witnessed two days of the worst combat ever in U.S. history. This brings us to September 17, 1862, when combat between North and South swirled around another humble house of worship in the bloodiest one-day battle in American history. Antietam's Dunker Church competes with the Alamo and Shiloh Church as the ranking house of worship in our military history.

Until now, no single book has been dedicated to a study of this modest historic edifice. The seminal works of historian John Schildt have certainly laid the ground work for a better understanding of the church and the Dunkers. The National Park Service produced a handout that provided a basic outline history of the church under the direction of Park Ranger Betty Otto. Mrs. Otto was a member of the local Brethren congregation in Sharpsburg descended from the original Dunker Church. She deserves much credit for promoting the history of the Dunker Church during her tenure on the staff of Antietam National Battlefield. As volunteer coordinator, she coordinated a team of teens and pre-teens affectionately known as the "Dunkets." These young people manned the church on weekends in period costume while interpreting its history. I have a particular interest in this group since my daughter Rica was one of them. (She has gone on to a successful career with the National Park Service.) Both John Schildt and Betty Otto are to be commended for laying the foundation for our understanding of both the Dunkers and the church.

Why should you read this book? First, this really is an outstanding study of Antietam's Dunker Church. I hesitate to use the word "definitive" because other information about it will almost certainly surface in the future. However, it is a complete history that examines the roots of the "Dunker" movement in Europe, the early years in America, and its establishment in the Antietam Valley. The authors take the reader on a journey through the battle, some postwar reunions, the destruction of the church in a windstorm, commemorations, the churches' reconstruction, and its value as a battlefield shrine.

The other major reason for reading and owning this book are the authors. Alann Schmidt has spent more than a decade researching the history of the church. His hard work has discovered rare accounts of the battle of Antietam and the church. Terry Barkley brings to the table a vast knowledge of church history from the Reformation to the present. Collectively, Alann and Terry are the leading authorities on the Dunker Church of Antietam Battlefield.

This is an essential volume for all students of the Battle of Antietam, the American Civil War, and the religious history of America.

Ted Alexander
Historian (Retired)
Antietam National Battlefield

Introduction

The Battle of Antietam, or Sharpsburg as it was known in the South, was fought on Wednesday, September 17, 1862, on the rolling landscape along Antietam Creek. By the time the sun went down, 23,100 men, North and South, had been killed, wounded or were missing. It was the bloodiest single day of the Civil War, and remains the bloodiest day in our history because every man who fought at Antietam was an American. In fact, more Americans fell there than in the Revolution, War of 1812, Mexican War, and Spanish-American War combined.

In the very midst of this harvest of death stood a little whitewashed meetinghouse of the German Baptist Brethren, or Dunkers (Dunkards), as they were colloquially known. Built in 1853 and known as the Mumma Church of the Manor congregation, the edifice was only about ten years old at the time of the battle. It was a house of worship dedicated to peace, equality, and to the brotherhood of all men—all to the glory of God. The irony of the situation is palpable.

Before the mighty armies moved away from the battlefield, the Dunker Church (as it would forever come to be known) would serve as a first aid station, a hospital—something akin to a modern-day triage center for immediate medical care where numerous amputations were performed—a morgue, an embalming station, and a temporary cemetery. The home of Samuel Mumma, the Dunker who donated the land for the church, would serve none of these purposes, for it was burned to the ground during the battle.

General Thomas J. "Stonewall" Jackson may have made the Dunker Church his headquarters just before the battle. Clara Barton, the "Angel of the Battlefield," reportedly visited the church to remove some of the wounded to other field hospitals. President Abraham Lincoln likely stopped at the little meetinghouse while touring the battlefield in early October 1862, giving a brief talk from its steps and visiting inside with the wounded of both armies. And, as you will read in the appendix entitled "Antietam's Dunker Church: A Tactical Overview," by Ted Alexander, the Antietam National Battlefield's former chief historian, Confederate Generals Jeb Stuart and John Bell Hood had made the Dunker Church their temporary headquarters before the battle.

All of this is only the beginning of the remarkable story of the Dunker Church at Antietam, one that would eventually include a stolen holy relic, disastrous souvenir hunting, a windstorm so bad it would destroy the historic structure, and even the tangential involvement of Samuel Langhorne Clemens, better known to us as Mark Twain.

Today, the Dunker Church stands as one of the most iconic structures of the Civil War and as a major tourist stop on the Antietam battlefield. It remains a beacon of peace as well as a beacon of hope for all—a symbol to the world of the good that is in all mankind.

Terry Barkley
Deavers Alley
Lexington, Virginia
May 15, 2017

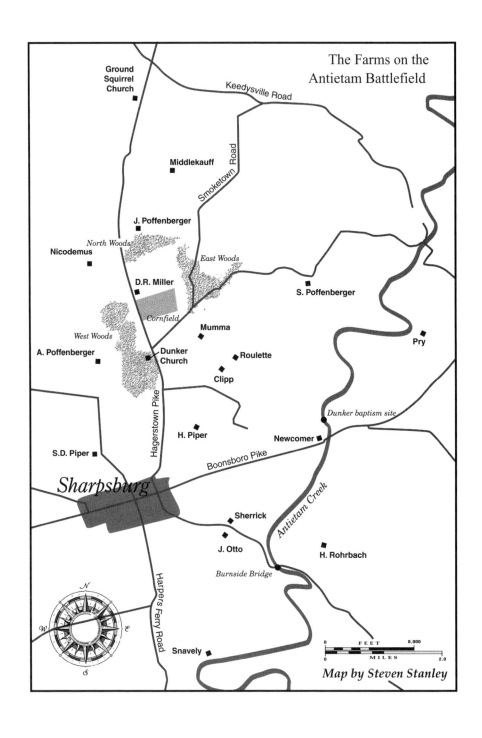

The Farms on the
Antietam Battlefield

Ground Squirrel Church

Keedysville Road

Middlekauff

Smoketown Road

J. Poffenberger

North Woods

Nicodemus

East Woods

D.R. Miller

S. Poffenberger

Cornfield

West Woods

Mumma

Pry

A. Poffenberger

Dunker Church

Roulette

Clipp

Dunker baptism site

Hagerstown Pike

H. Piper

Newcomer

S.D. Piper

Boonsboro Pike

Sharpsburg

Antietam Creek

Sherrick

J. Otto

H. Rohrbach

Burnside Bridge

N

W

E

S

Harper's Ferry Road

Snavely

FEET   8,000
0
0   MILES   2.0

Map by Steven Stanley

Chapter 1

Who are these Dunkers?

The German Baptist Brethren was founded in Schwarzenau, Wittgestein, Germany, in August 1708, forged from a melding of both Anabaptist and Radical Pietist influences in the wake of the Protestant Reformation in Europe. Its founders, eight believers seeking religious freedom—five men and three women, most were under the age of thirty—were baptized by immersion in the Eder River. They referred to themselves simply as "Brethren."

Alexander Mack, a miller by trade, was the organizer and first minister of these "New Baptists," who beginning in 1908 would be called the Church of the Brethren. The locals in Schwarzenau referred to these new believers as Neu-Taufer (New Baptists); "taufen" in German means "to baptize." They were also frequently called "Tunkers" (Dunkers in English), based on the German word "tunken" ("to dip") because their mode of baptism immersed candidates under water three times in the names of the Holy Trinity.

The Brethren formed as a dissenting group outside of the three traditions (Roman Catholic, Lutheran, and Reformed churches) legally established by the Treaty of Westphalia, which closed the Thirty Years' War (1618-1648). People who did not conform to doctrinal statements and practice of one of the legally established religions were persecuted as heretics. The small group of Brethren gathered in Schwarzenau would surely have faced legal penalties were it not for the toleration offered by the count of Wittgenstein. The insistence of the Brethren to evangelize and baptize adults, however, made it impossible for the Count to shield them from the wrath of other rulers. Tired of the persecution and seeking economic opportunity in the

Painting of the first Dunker baptisms in Schwarzenau, Germany, August 1708, by H. Durkee (1958), which hangs in the Brethren Historical Library and Archives (BHLA) in Elgin, IL. *BHLA*

New World, the Brethren accepted William Penn's invitation to move across the Atlantic Ocean and settle in Pennsylvania, where they would be free to practice their religious convictions. Elder Peter Becker led the first group of Brethren to the New World in 1719, where they settled in Germantown, seven miles northwest of Philadelphia. The largest group immigrated to Germantown ten years later, led by Alexander Mack, who died there in 1735.[1]

A year before Mack's group arrived, Conrad Beissel, a Brethren minister of the Conestoga congregation in Lancaster County, Pennsylvania, broke away from the Brethren. In 1732 he formed his own group, the

---

1   Donald F. Duenbaugh, ed., "Church of the Brethren," in *The Brethren Encyclopedia* 3 vols. (Philadelphia, PA, 1983), vol. 1, 298-305; Ronald J. Gordon, "Little Dunker Church: A Silent Witness for Peace," Church of the Brethren Network, August 1988, last updated March 2013. www.cob-net.org/antietam/.

A typical baptism of the Dunkers, this one in 1905 in Stony Creek in the Shenandoah Valley of Virginia. Charles Nesselrodt is performing the baptism. *BHLA*

Ephrata community, at Ephrata, Pennsylvania. These believers took Saturday as their day of worship and practiced a mystical form of Christianity promoting celibacy and a largely vegetarian diet. After the last Ephrata celibates died in 1813, the remaining community reorganized as the German Seventh Day Baptists. An offshoot of Ephrata, the Snow Hill Community (Nunnery), formed in Quincy Township near Waynesboro, Pennsylvania.

The Brethren did not issue any definitive creedal statements, choosing instead to accept the New Testament as their only "rule of faith and practice" while professing an almost literal interpretation of the Scriptures. They practiced believer's baptism by trine immersion, the consecration of Christian workers by the laying on of hands, the anointing of the sick, and the complete love feast service consisting of foot-washing, a fellowship meal, and the Holy Communion.[2]

2   Jeff Bach, *Voices of the Turtledoves: The Sacred World of Ephrata* (University Park, PA, 2003); Denise A. Seachrist, *Snow Hill: In the Shadows of the Ephrata Cloister* (Kent, OH, 2010). H. Austin Cooper and Arthur Scrogum, "The Dunker Church and the Church of

The Brethren believed that repentance and the baptism of believers was required for a true Christian life and for salvation. They professed "love and service, in place of war, as Christ's message." The Brethren rejected infant baptism in favor of adult baptism, when the applicant could choose whether to be baptized and become a member of the Brethren church. They believed that only adults could fully comprehend the significance and the "cost" of the baptismal ceremony.[3]

Baptism was by forward trine immersion, usually in a flowing stream like Jesus' baptism in the Jordan River, the believer being completely immersed three times "in the name of the Father, the Son, and the Holy Ghost." At the time of the Battle of Antietam in 1862, the Dunkers were known as the German Baptist Brethren. Members referred to one another as "Brother" or "Sister" or simply, "Brethren."[4]

The Dunkers believed in the equality and brotherhood of all men and that slavery and war were abominations to a truly Christian life. The Brethren preferred the simple life and adhered to the Biblical admonition to be in the world, but not of the world.[5]

Following Jesus' example of overcoming evil with good, the Dunkers shied away from litigation and lawsuits—"going to law"—preferring instead to follow the Biblical example of handling such matters within the church body. They also refused to swear oaths, often only "affirming" like the Quakers and other similar groups. The Brethren held that if one were honest and sincere in their conduct and words, there would be no need for oaths. They swore allegiance only to God.

The old Brethren prohibited Sunday Schools and even musical instruments in their churches. The long list of "don'ts" (as opposed to a short

---

the Brethren," The Middle Maryland District and the General Brotherhood Board of the Church of the Brethren, pamphlet, undated.

3   A favorite Brethren hymn by Alexander Mack, Jr., is "Count Well the Cost, When You Lay the Foundation."

4   "40th Annual Dunker Church Worship Service," September 19, 2010, Antietam National Battlefield, Sharpsburg, Maryland, sponsored by Churches of the Brethren in Maryland and West Virginia," booklet. This annual commemorative worship service was held on the Sunday after the anniversary of the battle, the closest Sunday to the battle's anniversary.

5   "The Dunker Church," Antietam National Battlefield Site (U. S. Department of the Interior, National Park Service, undated), 1-2 of 8-page booklet.

approved list) included the partaking of strong drink, women praying without prayer veils, having their images taken or "stolen" (like the Amish), and, apparently, even working as a butcher in a market.[6]

Until the early 1880s, the Brethren were generally of one body and of like minds. The "great schisms" of 1880-1882 over doctrinal differences shattered that unity, when several groups broke away from the main body of the German Baptist Brethren (now known as the Church of the Brethren). The most conservative group became the Old German Baptist Brethren, and the progressives became The Brethren Church. A smaller group of about 1,000 followers left the Church of the Brethren in 1926 to become the Dunkard Brethren. Since then, other splinter groups have broken away from the three main bodies and have formed their own denominations to profess their beliefs and practices.

The most conservative members emphasized consistency, obedience, and the order of the Brethren. They opposed the use of musical instruments, Sunday Schools, and worldly amusements. They promoted plain dress, simple living, and church discipline. The progressives in the church focused on grace and acceptance. They promoted higher education, salaried ministers, Sunday Schools, and revivalism. The majority of Brethren held a position between these two extremes.[7]

The Brethren congregations of the eighteenth and nineteenth centuries were served by a plural free ministry (more than one unsalaried minister) with three degrees of ministry, the eldership being the highest degree. First and second degree ministers were ministers in training that would lead to eventual ordination. Elders were chosen from the ordained ministers (second degree) after years of good and faithful service:

> [Elders] were men whom congregations had selected to lead them, men 'set apart' by persons intimately familiar with their character, competencies, and spirituality. Called to the ministry by their local churches, they were confirmed as elders by District Elders' Bodies that had likewise become familiar with the quality of their service.

6 Kathleen A. Ernst, *Too Afraid To Cry: Maryland Civilians in the Antietam Campaign* (Mechanicsburg, PA, 1999), 13.

7 Church of the Brethren: https://en.wikipedia.org/wiki/Church_of_the_Brethren; "Church of the Brethren," *The Brethren Encyclopedia*, vol. 1, 1983, 298-305.

In a word, to be an elder was to be honored by one's home community and one's fellow ministers. It was the supreme recognition of one's spirituality and faithfulness to the church. Elders could be both gentle and stern; respected and feared. They wielded tremendous authority in the life of the church, more through their ability to sway a congregation than through any absolutist powers attached to their office. On virtually any church matter, they could theoretically be overruled by the members of church council. That they often had their way is a testimony to their personal influence and esteem in their communities. They had, after all, been called to be housekeepers, and they were expected to exercise authority in the congregation. Unlike the professional pastors who began to make their presence widely felt during the twenties [1920s], the qualifications of elders were solely spiritual, their religious studies were self-initiated and self-directed, and their rewards were nonmaterial. The eldership was the highest degree of the Dunker free-ministry, a system that had prompted earlier generations to boast that Brethren gave 'the Bread of Life, the message of common salvation unto all men without money or price.'

The eldership was finally abolished within the Church of the Brethren in 1967 in favor of a college-educated, seminary-trained professional pastorate.[8]

The Brethren regard the Dunker Church of Antietam Battlefield as "an eternal symbol of peace on the site of the bloodiest single-day battle of the Civil War." The Brethren hope "that the little white church on the Antietam battlefield may be to our troubled world a symbol of tolerance, love, brotherhood, and service—a witness to the mind and spirit of Him whom we seek to serve.[9]

The Church of the Brethren is recognized by the Federal government as one of the "Historic Peace Churches" along with the Mennonites and the

---

8 Carl F. Bowman, *Brethren Society: The Cultural Transformation of a "Peculiar People"* (Baltimore, MD, 1995), 301; "Ministry," *The Brethren Encyclopedia*, vol. 2, 844-845; "Elder," *The Brethren Encyclopedia*, vol. 1, 432; Terry Barkley, *One Who Served: Brethren Elder Charles Nesselrodt of Shenandoah County, Virginia* (Staunton, VA, 2004), 42-44.

9 Cooper and Scrogum, "The Dunker Church and the Church of the Brethren"; "40th Annual Dunker Church Worship Service."

Quakers (Society of Friends). These centuries-old churches believe that the New Testament forbids Christian involvement in violence and war. As such, most members of these "peace churches" are pacifists and many are conscientious objectors against serving in the military.

Chapter 2

The Brethren Come
to the Antietam Valley

The original settlers to the region in the mid-eighteenth century were the so-called "Pennsylvania Germans" or "Deutsche" (Pennsylvania Dutch). While many were Mennonites, a "Plain People" or "Sect People" like the Dunkers and the Amish, they were a minority. As many as 90% of the Germans who came to the New World were "Church People" of the Lutheran and Reformed faiths.[1]

When western Maryland opened for settlement, Dunkers and those of the Lutheran and Reformed faiths in eastern Pennsylvania crossed the mountains moving west and south by southwest, finally planting their roots in the Antietam Valley. About 1740, German Baptist Brethren began settling along the Conococheague and Antietam Creeks in Maryland. Initially worshiping in their own homes, by 1751 the Brethren organized a congregation known as Conococheague or Antietam. The Conococheague church, which included all the territory of the Cumberland and Antietam Valleys down to the Potomac River west of the Blue Ridge, became the first permanent organization of the Brethren west of the Blue Ridge Mountains. Its membership lived in Pennsylvania and Maryland, though there appeared to be more members living in Maryland. Springing from this large

---

1 "The Dunker Church: A Battlefield Shrine," undated and unnumbered 4-page National Park Service teaching tool with questions for students, 1.

congregation came the Beaver Creek, Brownsville, Manor, Mumma [Dunker Church], Hagerstown, and Sharpsburg Churches.[2]

By 1742, Elder Abraham Stouffer had organized the Antietam congregation near Waynesboro, Pennsylvania, just across the Maryland-Pennsylvania line. Stouffer had been ordained in Germantown, Pennsylvania, by Peter Becker, the first Brethren elder in America. A large portion of the Antietam or Conococheague congregation lived in Maryland. In 1750, Elder George Adam Martin became the presiding elder, and in 1785, Elder John Price built the first church near Waynesboro, known as the Upper Antietam or Price Church. Elder Price was followed by Elder Nicholas Martin and then Elder Daniel Reichard in 1830, the year the Manor Church was built—the "Mother Church" of the little Dunker Church of Antietam Battlefield.

The Manor Church of the German Baptist Brethren was one of the earliest meetinghouses of the denomination built west of the Susquehanna River and south of the Pennsylvania line. It was located in Washington County, Maryland, two miles east of Tilghmanton and about midway between Sharpsburg and Hagerstown. The foundation was laid in 1829 and construction was completed the next year. The church, which is still in use today, was built of limestone rock collected from Dunker John Leonard Emmert's neighboring farm.

The Manor Church grew rapidly under the leadership of Elders Daniel Reichard, Jacob Long, David Long, and Daniel Wolf. The 1838 and 1857 Annual Conferences of the German Baptist Brethren were held there. As the membership continued to grow, other church edifices were built within the bounds and limits of "The Manor" until it held ministerial leadership over four meetinghouses: the Marsh Church, Mumma [Dunker] Church, Potomac Church or Downsville Church and, much later, the Sharpsburg Church, which opened in 1899. "Love Feast," including Holy Communion, for these churches was held in the Manor Church, where several hundred people, including non-Brethren "friends," attended the festivities surrounding the solemn but joyous religious gathering.

---

2   J. Maurice Henry, *History of the Church of the Brethren in Maryland* (Elgin, IL, 1936), 176; Cooper and Scrogum, "The Dunker Church and the Church of the Brethren"; Ernst, *Too Afraid To Cry*, 59.

The Manor Church of the Brethren, the "Mother Church" of the Mumma Church (Dunker Church), near Tilghmanton, MD, four miles northeast of the Antietam battlefield. *Dr. Jeff Bach*

The first of The Manor's offspring was the Marsh Church built about 1849 on Rench Road two miles south of Hagerstown. Preaching was conducted in the 35' x 40' brick structure for more than thirty years until the building was sold and the work transferred elsewhere. The second church was the Mumma [Dunker] Church completed in 1853, and the Potomac Church near Downsville built in 1859. Located four miles west of The Manor, the Downsville Church was a 30' x 40' brick structure.[3]

The German Baptist Brethren were not the dominant religious denomination in Washington County and the Sharpsburg area. In fact, most of the Germans in this region were members of the Lutheran and Reformed

3   "The Manor Church of the Brethren, Mother of the Dunkard Church of Antietam Battlefield," a two-page unsigned document produced by the Manor Church; Henry, *History of the Church of the Brethren in Maryland*, 176-179, 191-193; Thomas J. C. Williams, *A History of Washington County, Maryland* (Baltimore, MD, 1968), 523-528. When planning for the reconstruction of the Dunker Church on Antietam battlefield, which was accomplished in 1962, the architecture and building materials of the various church structures of the Manor congregation and other period Brethren churches were examined. See report by Ranger-Historian Louis E. Tuckerman, Antietam National Battlefield Site.

churches. Many Civil War buffs assume that nearly all of the farms on Antietam battlefield with anglicized Germanic names were Dunkers, but that is not the case. The Mumma, Sherrick, Otto, and Neikirk families were German Baptist Brethren at the time of the battle (and a case can be made that David R. (D. R.) Miller, whose farm (including the infamous Cornfield) was just up Hagerstown Pike from the Mumma or Dunker Church, was as well). Other farms may also have been Brethren, though they constituted a small but important and visible minority.[4]

Dunker settlement in the beautiful and fertile Antietam Valley was fortuitous. Founded in 1776, Washington County in western Maryland was the first in the nation to be named after George Washington. It is also one of three Maryland counties considered to be part of Appalachia because the of its location in the Appalachian Mountains (Blue Ridge).[5]

Sharpsburg, the first town in Washington County, was laid out in 1763 by Joseph Chapline just east of the Potomac River 13 miles south of Hagerstown. Sharpsburg was in competition with Hagerstown to be the county seat, but lost by only one vote. Ironically, its loss ensured the village (which had 1,200-1,300 people during the Civil War and only 706 in 2014) would remain mostly pristine, free of the urban sprawl and development that has spread across so many parts of Maryland. (Hagerstown, for example, has a current population of more than 40,000.) In the long run, this single vote probably saved the Antietam battlefield from almost certain destruction.[6]

---

4 "The Dunker Church: A Battlefield Shrine," 1; Kevin M. Walker and K. C. Kirkman, *Antietam Farmsteads: A Guide to the Battlefield Landscape* (Sharpsburg, MD, 2010), 59, 71, 94, 102. Little is known about the David R. Miller family, one of the half-dozen original families of the Mumma Church. Samuel Mumma's second wife was a Miller. Given the proximity of the D. R. Miller farm to the Dunker Church and the Mumma and Roulette farms, it is reasonable to suspect that he was a Dunker, if not a good one. Rev. H. Austin Cooper suspected that Miller was indeed a Dunker.

5 Washington County, Maryland: http://washco-md.net/. The present population of the county is nearly 150,000 people.

6 Freeman Ankrum, *Sidelights on Brethren History* (Elgin, IL, 1962), 100; Sharpsburg, Maryland: http://sharpsburgmd.com/; Vernell Doyle and Tim Doyle, *Sharpsburg* (Charleston, SC, 2009); Hagerstown, Maryland: www.hagerstownmd.org/; Mary H. Rubin, *Hagerstown* (Charleston, SC, 2001); *Battle of Antietam Centennial and Hagerstown Bicentennial: Official Program and Historical Guide, Aug. 31 Through Sept. 17, 1962* (Washington County and Frederick County, MD, 1962), 72. James Rumsey, who invented the steamboat, once lived in Sharpsburg, and British General Edward Braddock slept there on his ill-fated military expedition to western Pennsylvania in 1755.

Chapter 3

A Dunker Presence
in the Sharpsburg Area

On February 22, 1851, Samuel and Elizabeth (Miller) Mumma, members of the German Baptist Brethren, "sold" a small portion of their 182 and 1/4-acre farm known as "Anderson's Delight" to seven deacons of the local German Baptist Brethren congregation for the nominal sum of $10. The purpose of the "sale" was so the Brethren could build their own a meetinghouse on it. The Dunkers had been meeting various Brethren homes and barns in the area, including Daniel Miller's north of Sharpsburg.

The donated plot totaled 100 perches or .6 of an acre (though the reported acreage varies). The land fronted the west side of the dirt road running from Sharpsburg to Hagerstown, what we know today as the Hagerstown Pike, which was not open until 1856. The little church would be built facing east, and the site itself is west of the Samuel Mumma (pronounced Moo-maw) farmhouse, outbuildings, and cemetery. The Indenture (deed) listed the deacons (grantees) as Joseph Wolf, John S. Rowland, Samuel Fahrney, Jacob Reichard, Samuel Emmert, John W. Stoufer, and Valentine Reichard. It specifically designated that the land be used for the building of a church, "ordained as aforesaid forever, and to and for no other use intent or purpose whatsoever."

The deed continued as follows:

Samuel and Elizabeth (Miller) Mumma donated the land in 1851 for the Mumma Church (Dunker Church). Their home was the only one destroyed during the battle on September 17, 1862. *Antietam National Battlefield (ANB), Sharpsburg, MD*

. . . the Church who call themselves Brethren, having and considering the Holy Scriptures alone as the object of their faith, and holding and professing the New Testament solely as the rule for their church government, and for their religious practices, renouncing and disavowing all other creeds, men's confessions of faith, and elder traditions; preferring and professing the deciding, determining, and squaring all church matters by and with the New Testament.

Interestingly, the deed further stated that the church building could be used by other Christian denominations for their funerals as long as this did not interfere with special Brethren religious gatherings:

A faded postwar view of the Dunker Church at the intersection of Hagerstown Pike and Smoketown Road. *ANB*

. . . then all other Christian denominations shall have the privilege, on funeral occasions, when they bury their dead in the burying ground on the aforesaid tract of land called Anderson's Delight, and known as Mumma's graveyard, to have the use of such house of public worship to hold therein their funeral devotions, and preach therein their funeral sermons, provided such devotions do not interfere with or hinder any meeting especially appointed for holding Lovefeast and communion by said Church of Brethren, and that the aforesaid hundred perches of land only be used by the aforesaid Church of Brethren to erect thereon a house for public worship and for the convenience of holding there their religious services.[1]

1   The Indenture (deed) was recorded at the request of Joseph Wolf on April 2, 1851, as Land Record Liber IN 5 50, page 686. It is unclear whether the use of the Mumma meetinghouse and Mumma cemetery by other Christian denominations was a purely magnanimous gesture on the part of the zealous Samuel and Elizabeth Mumma, or whether a charge or donation for non-Brethren use was expected. As it turned out, because of the throng of people who attended Love Feast, it was only held in the Manor Church.

The church site was on a slight rocky rise at the western corner of the Mumma property about a mile north of Sharpsburg at the juncture of the dirt road to Hagerstown (Hagerstown Pike) and the Smoketown Road, two thoroughfares that would play a major role during the Battle of Antietam. The building of the Mumma meetinghouse of the Manor congregation began in 1852 and the edifice was completed and dedicated to the Lord in 1853. Daniel Miller, Samuel Mumma's father-in-law, who donated the altar Bible to the congregation in 1851, and Joseph Sherrick supervised the construction. John Eacker (Ecker), Joseph Sherry, and George Peterman, a skilled carpenter, completed and furnished the interior of the church.

Rev. H. Austin Cooper, a former pastor of the Sharpsburg Church of the Brethren in the 1940s and a scholar on the subject writing a book about the Dunker Church, recorded that the building committee included Elder Daniel Miller, Joseph Sherrick, John Ecker, Henry F. Neikirk, and Samuel Creamer. "The woodwork of the building," continued Cooper, "was done by Noah and John Putnam. Samuel Creamer was the mason and directed that work. These brick were made and burned on the John Otto farm . . . near Burnside Bridge, in the field near the 11th Ohio Infantry monument. It is said that the original cost of the building was $845."[2]

The Mumma or Dunker Church was a single-story, one-room brick vernacular structure with a gabled roof. The little whitewashed church was and nearly square and measured 35' 6" long by 34' 6" wide, and about 24' high   (some say 35' x 40'). It was built entirely by members of the congregation, many of whom were craftsmen and artisans. It was common practice for them to help each other build homes, barns, and outbuildings. Wood was hewn on local Dunker wood lots and handmade clay bricks for the walls were fired in earthen kilns on the John David Otto farm (a Lutheran), and possibly on Joseph Poffenberger's farm.[3] The heavier beams

---

2   Rev. H. Austin Cooper, "A Brief Sketch of the Development of the Reconstruction Project, 1960-1962," (New Windsor, MD, August 31, 1962), written for the "Antietam Battlefield Dunker Church Rededication, September 2, 1962," one of four typed pages.

3   A great-grandson of John David Otto's was Brethren Elder John E. Otto, the last minister of the little Dunker Church; John W. Schildt, *Drums Along the Antietam* (Parsons, WV, 1972), 288; Williams, *A History of Washington County, Maryland*, 527; Alann Schmidt, draft, *Historic American Buildings Survey, Dunker Church, Antietam National Battlefield*, np; E. Russell Hicks, "The Church on the Battlefield," part one, *Gospel Messenger* (February 2, 1952), 9.

Post-battle Dunker Church image by Alexander Gardner. Note the solid color door and shutters and post- and rail-fence along the Hagerstown Pike. LOC

and timbers for the church were hewn with a broadax, and timber was sawed into boards at a mill on the banks of Antietam Creek. The boards used for the flooring were tongue-in-groove, and those used for the doors and window frames were hand-finished.[4]

The exterior of the Dunker Church was a plain whitewashed brick building with green shutters and doors and a wood-shingled roof. There was no steeple, no cross, no stained glass windows or other architectural decoration or ornamentation. At the time, there was not even any signage. The building sat on a fieldstone foundation. The small white structure was a focal point during the morning phase of the fierce battle in September 1862, and many soldiers mistook it for a farmhouse or a country or district school.

The main entrance of the church faced east toward the Hagerstown Pike a handful of yards distant. Another door was cut in the south wall, which also contained the two gable windows illuminating the attic. The ground floor had two large shuttered windows in each of the four walls. The wooden

---

4   Robert L. Lagemann, Antietam park historian, *Historic Structures Report For the Dunkard Church, Antietam National Battlefield Site, May 25, 1960*, 9, 11, 15-16, 57, 59-60; "The Dunkard Church" (National Park Service: Antietam National Battlefield, revised 1965); Arnold S. Platou, *After the Dunker Church . . . A Century of Faithful Service: The Sharpsburg Church of the Brethren, 1899-1999* (Sharpsburg, MD, 1999), 3, 6.

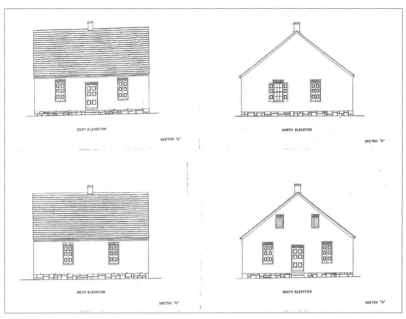

Architectural drawings of each elevation of the Dunker Church from Louis E. Tuckerman's 1951 report. *ANB*

shingle roof was pierced in its center by a brick chimney supported by a platform on the attic floor level. Heat was supplied by two iron stoves near the center of the main floor. The interior furnishings consisted primarily of twenty-two wooden benches with backs and an altar table. The church had no organ nor any other musical instrument.[5]

5 Lagemann, *Historic Structures Report For the Dunkard Church, Antietam National Battlefield Site, May 25, 1960*, 31, 59. Rev. Austin Cooper was told by at least one member of the Mumma Church who witnessed the battle that the original color of the doors and shutters was green, including solid green doors. The oldest available images of the church tend to bear this out, as the "front" or east door is a solid color; the "side" or south door probably was as well. In his 1960 report, p. 31, Robert Lagemann wrote: "most of the exterior woodwork was painted green, the typical 'shutter green' shade. This included the shutters throughout and the heavy parts of the doors." However, he added, "the panels of the doors were painted white, as were the door and window frames." This postwar green and white (later, gray and white) "abomination" [Cooper] is visible in images of the period. According to Rev. Cooper, the Civil War-era Dunkers would not have allowed such colorful painting on the doors. When the reconstructed Dunker Church was opened in 1962 on the original foundation, the doors were painted a solid gray. Later, the tacky two-color paint scheme reappeared.

Candles were used for interior lighting (later, kerosene lamps), while the large windows provided ample natural light. There was only one iron stove in the meetinghouse at the time of the battle (which is reflected today in the reconstructed Dunker Church on Antietam Battlefield).

The original congregation consisted of about a half-dozen farm families —the Mummas, Eckers (Eakers), Millers, Neikirks, Sherricks, and, later, the Ottos. Each accepted member had to first affirm that they would not own slaves and that they would not participate in war. However, the 1860 census for Sharpsburg reveals that several Brethren farmers owned slaves, including Samuel Mumma, who freed or manumitted his one remaining slave, and John Otto, who owned a slave woman and her son, both of whom he freed just after Lincoln's Emancipation Proclamation was issued (even though Maryland did not secede from the Union and was exempt from the proclamation). Some of the freed slaves decided to remain with, and work for, their former masters, which at least implies they had been treated reasonably well by the Dunkers. (The issue of slavery was considered as difficult and complex among some of the Brethren as it was in wider society.) New members were baptized on the Sharpsburg side of Antietam Creek, about midway along the farm lane north from the Middle Bridge to the Joseph Parks farm near a little bend in the creek.[6]

In a reflection of a typical German Baptist Brethren worship service of that time, the members of the Mumma congregation arrived early on Sunday morning for the worship service. The men entered the "front" or east door and sat on the right side, while the women and children entered the "side" or south door and sat on the left side facing the preachers' table at the front of the room. The women wore "prayer veils" or "prayer coverings," a small white cloth head-covering, and a black bonnet to cover the prayer covering. The bonnet was typically removed after entering the meeting house. Their dark-colored dresses were simple and featured high necks, long sleeves, and full-length skirts. A specially designed "handkerchief" hung over the front of their dresses covering their bosoms. Jewelry of any kind was strictly

---

6 Ernst, *Too Afraid To Cry*, 13-14, 243n28; Henry, *History of the Church of the Brethren in Maryland*, 192; Williams, *A History of Washington County, Maryland*, 527; Rev. Austin Cooper of the Church of the Brethren pointed out this site to co-author Terry Barkley about 1980. A visit in 2016 revealed drastic changes from its earlier appearance. The once-gentle slope has been washed away by flooding and erosion, and the grade is now so steep that cattle can no longer leave the pasture to drink in the creek there.

David R. and Margaret Miller. Their cornfield would become infamous as one of the bloodiest pieces of ground of the entire Civil War. *ANB*

forbidden, for gold and silver were considered "signals to Satan." As in most Brethren congregations, the women did much of the actual work on Sunday mornings. This included preparing all the food for meals in the homes after worship, and caring for the children.[7]

The men wore broad-brimmed hats atop their rounded haircuts, and sported bushy untrimmed beards. They usually wore dark coats, some without lapels (just a standing or upright collar). This "uniform" of sorts for the Brethren and other "Plain People" groups wasn't standard until after the Civil War. Brethren wore the same everyday clothing as others outside the faith, most of it being handmade at home. The clothing depicted in images of

---

7   Esther Fern Rupel, *Brethren Dress: A Testimony to Faith* (Philadelphia, PA, 1994). The "women's fellowship" in most Brethren congregations is a real power-base and nothing really gets done without their support!

Samuel and Elizabeth Mumma and David R. and Margaret Miller offer some insight into their dress. The men are non-Brethren in their appearance, but the women were dressed in a manner acceptable to the Dunkers.[8]

The most devout members of the congregation (something like an "Amen Corner") sat in the front of the church with the deacons occupying pews directly facing the preachers' table, sometimes referred to erroneously

8   "The Dunker Church, Antietam National Battlefield," 2-4; Walker and Kirkman, *Antietam Farmsteads: A Guide to the Battlefield Landscape*, 32 - 41; Ernst, *Too Afraid To Cry*m 120, 134; David R. (D. R.) Miller may have been a Dunker, though definitive evidence is lacking. His father was a militia colonel in the War of 1812. Rev. Perhaps, like Samuel Mumma, D. R. Miller came to the German Baptist Brethren from the (German) Reformed faith.

(Opposite top) Looking north of the Middle Bridge toward the Joseph Parks farm in this 1862 Alexander Gardner image, the baptism site for the Dunkers is just south of the Parks farm near the grove of trees on the Sharpsburg side of Antietam Creek. *LOC* (Opposite bottom) The Dunker baptism site in 1980 as pointed out by Rev. Austin Cooper. *Terry Barkley* (Above) The Dunker baptism site today is greatly altered from its 1980 appearance. Looking toward the Middle Bridge. *Dr. Jeff Bach*

as the pulpit table. Behind the preachers' table, facing the table and the congregation, sat the presiding elder and visiting elders and ministers (preachers). The Brethren enjoyed a plural free ministry (multiple ministers who served unsalaried for life) that served the Manor Church (with its mission or preaching points including the Mumma, Potomac, Marsh, and much later, Sharpsburg churches).

The preacher's table was a plain wooden affair upon which lay the opened Bible donated to the church by Daniel Miller. This was used in public worship with individual ministers often reading from their own Bibles before preaching. Because the old Brethren wanted everything on the same level, the chosen ministry were not raised higher than the congregation they served; all members of the church were considered "ministers." According to Miss Ruth Otto, a member of the congregation, an earthenware pitcher of water and several glasses were provided for the presiding elder and the other ministers. "Sometimes the sermon was rather lengthy,"

The interior of the Dunker Church illustrates the simplicity and the humbleness of the Civil War-era Brethren. *ANB*

explained Miss Otto, "and the speaker needed a drink of water to moisten his throat." The worship services, usually held once a month at each of the churches of the Manor congregation, could last for hours and included multiple sermons and hymn-singing without musical accompaniment.[9]

Ruth Otto was the daughter of Elder John E. Otto, the last minister of the Dunker Church who died in 1916. She attended the Mumma Church from the time she was a baby. Her reflections stem from her experiences in the late nineteenth and early twentieth centuries. Her recollections of the church and its furnishings, its members, and the services are invaluable. Regarding the benches or pews:

> The benches having just a plank as a back rest had quite a space between
> the seat and the back, so if a child went to sleep sometimes he fell through

---

9   Ruth Otto, "What I Remember About Dunker Church" (Sharpsburg, MD, February 6, 1962), np, in Rev. H. Austin Cooper Collection, Brethren Historical Library and Archives, Church of the Brethren General Offices, Elgin, IL; "Ministry," *The Brethren Encyclopedia*, vol. 2, 845. "The absence of a platform or pulpit is a sign of humble service which has historically characterized the ministry of the [old Brethren]." Ibid.

and the thud would waken the parent who might have fallen asleep during the long service.[10]

The hymns were "lined," meaning the minister either read out or sang a couple of lines first, after which the congregation sang the same lines in unison. "We had no instrument and didn't always get the right pitch or tune," confessed Miss Otto, "but we sang with the spirit and sure made a joyful noise."[11]

Interestingly, no offering was collected during the worship service. Because ministers were not paid for their service to the congregation (hence the term, "free ministry"), there was no need to collect an offering for their salaries. If needs arose within the congregation, members donated money to help offset those needs.

The schedule of worship services within the Manor Church circuit was also something Miss Otto recalled:

> I was a regular attendant every four weeks. The appointment was every four weeks because there were four churches in the circuit. The Manor (the Mother Church), Downsville, the Marsh and the Mumma House. The presiding elder for that day would make this announcement. 'We will meet one week from today at the Manor. Two weeks at Downsville, Three weeks at the Marsh and Four weeks here again. The Lord willing.'[12]

She also noted that it was impossible to forget long-time Elders David Long and Daniel Wolf, "with their white beards and straight collared coats, I thought Moses must have looked like them."[13]

The Mumma Church served as a kind of community center for the little Dunker congregation in the Sharpsburg area. The long Sunday worship service and gatherings during the week provided ample time for fellowship, including meeting and greeting friends and visitors. Those traveling from a distance usually stayed in neighboring Brethren homes for the duration of

10 Otto, "What I Remember About Dunker Church."

11 Ibid.

12 Ibid.

13 Ibid.

"Love Feast among the Dunkers," by Howard Pyle, *Harper's Weekly*, March 17, 1883. *BHLA*

their visit. The Mumma Church included an attic, accessed by a ladder, with two windows on the south side of the building. There does not appear to be any evidence that Brethren, particularly children, were ever billeted there; it may have been used primarily for storage.

Church occasions, and especially Love Feast at the Manor Church, were excellent times for young people to meet. The children found new playmates, and teenagers and young people of the opposite sex met and interacted. Many future spouses were chosen in this manner, for the Brethren usually married other Brethren or someone from a similar pacifist religious body, like the Mennonites.

The most solemn and cherished ritual for the Brethren was and remains Love Feast, including the washing of feet, a simple bowl of soup, and Holy Communion—a commemoration of the Last Supper. Love Feast was usually held twice a year, typically in the fall and spring. Love Feast was always held in The Manor meetinghouse for that congregation, and for her three off-spring churches, including the Mumma congregation. More than 200 Brethren belonged to The Manor and her preaching points. Furthermore, some 200 to 300 people, including non- Brethren "friends" who were always welcome to attend the events, came to Love Feast though only baptized

"Double mode" of feetwashing among the Dunkers where one person washes the feet and another dries them. This was the mode of baptism used by the Dunkers during the Civil War period. Art work by G. W. Peters in an article by Nelson Lloyd, "Among the Dunkers," *Scribner's Magazine* (November 1901). *BHLA*

members of the Brethren could partake in the actual communion ceremony. The off-spring churches of The Manor were simply too small and ill-equipped to entertain such a throng.

Love Feast usually began with a sermon and a time of self-examination that included hymn-singing. The Brethren minister who opened the service rose and testified to the love and power of God. Thereafter, a minister read John 13 and preached about the meaning of feetwashing. While he preached, the deacons and their wives began the ritual.

It started when a member rose and tied a towel around his or her waist. Another member kneeled and, using a simple small tub of water, washed the feet of the man or woman sitting next to him or her. The member holding the towel dried the feet. The pair doing the washing and drying often served two people in this manner, greeting them with a handshake ("the right hand of fellowship") and with the "holy kiss of charity" (a light kiss on the lips). This procedure, called the "double mode" of feetwashing because two people performed the ritual, was repeated by those whose feet had just been washed and dried.

The process continued around the tables until everyone's feet had been washed and dried and each had received the right hand of fellowship and the "holy kiss." Separated by tables, men administered to the men while women did the same for the women, repeating the same procedure. After the feetwashing another short sermon was preached and a simple soup of lamb or beef was served to once more commemorate the Last Supper Jesus ate with his disciples. The actual communion ceremony followed with the impressive service ending with a closing hymn and a prayer.

Ruth Otto remembered that Love Feast at The Manor was held on Saturday and was typical of other Dunker churches in the Brotherhood. She went on to describe the "single mode" of feetwashing (which was not used by the Dunkers at the time of the Civil War):

After prayer and a hymn John 13 was read and the service of feet washing began. A little tub of water had been placed at the end of each table along with a big cotton flannel apron and a towel (the towel was dampened and reserved to be passed to wipe ones hands after their shoes and stockings were again donned). The apron was tied around the waist of one and then they washed the feet on the one next to them and wiped them with the apron, gave them a kiss of love and passed on the apron to be used on the next one. While this service was in progress one of the visiting ministers explained the service. It took quite a while when there were several hundred members present. When the service was completed the Deacons carried the tubs, aprons and towels to the basement and returned with large buckets of water and dippers to fill the glasses and others brought large kettles of hot broth to put in the dishes of broken bread. We sang hymns until everything was ready. After giving thanks for the meal we ate in silence, bread and butter, cold lamb and hot soup, and it tasted so good different from the meal at home. After supper the tables were again covered and one of the ministers read John 19 telling us of the suffering and death of our Lord. While that was being read the officiating minister would break the unleavened bread into strips and place it on piles to be distributed to the congregation. The men broke the bread to each other but a minister walked thro the isles and gave each woman a small piece repeating, 'This bread we break is the Communion of the body of Christ.' When all had been served a prayer was offered and it was eaten in silence.

The grape juice or fruit of the vine was in large glass bottles. It was poured into 2 silver cups and passed around each one taking a sip and saying, 'This cup of the New Testament is the Communion of the blood of Christ.' After this service was completed announcements were made and invitations given to other Love Feasts. We sang a hymn and went out, and it was night.[14]

The sick were anointed with oil by the elders and deacons who visited the Brethren farms in the area. Deaths were announced door to door by members of the congregation. Brethren funerals of an earlier period were rather simple affairs. The funeral of Alexander Mack, Sr., the organizer and first minister of the German Baptist Brethren who died in 1735, for example, entailed little more than a pine box prepared for the body, lined with a linen cloth and wood shavings. Ever superstitious, the Brethren carried the coffin to the funeral head-first with the feet pointing toward the door out of which the body would eventually be carried. A feast of gammon (cured ham),

14 Otto, ibid. The feetwashing ceremony described by Miss Otto is the "single mode," which was used in more modern times,where one person washes and dries the feet of the person next to them. The person just washed then performs the same procedure for the person next to them, and so on down the line. The "double mode" of feetwashing has one person washing the feet of the person next to them (or, perhaps, a couple of people at the same time) while a second person dries the feet of that person or persons. This moves the process along more quickly and is especially useful in larger congregations. Brethren historian Dr. Jeff Bach reports that the "single mode" of feetwashing was not used by the Dunkers at the time of the Civil War.

cheese, cakes, and punch was served at noon. The funeral cortege made its way to the cemetery only when night fell, perhaps chanting and singing along the way. When the coffin was lowered into the grave and half the dirt returned, the torches were thrown in and the rest of the dirt was used to fill the grave. It is not known if Brethren funerals conducted in the Mumma graveyard followed a similar pattern.[15]

The Mumma congregation was an active little church dedicated to nonviolence, equality, and the brotherhood of all men. It was only about ten-years-old when Hell erupted around it on what would be the bloodiest single day in American history.

---

15 "The Dunker Church," Antietam National Battlefield Site, 2-4; Julius F. Sachse, *German Sectarians of Pennsylvania*, 2 vols. (Philadelphia, PA, 1899), vol. 1, 217-222.

Chapter 4

When Eagles Collide:
A Brief Overview of America's Bloodiest Day

a host of books, magazine articles, and other publications have been written about the Maryland Campaign of 1862 and the Battle of Antietam. With the exception of Gettysburg, probably no other Civil War battle has been so deeply analyzed and discussed. What follows is simply a short overview of the major events surrounding the Battle of Antietam, Wednesday, September 17, 1862.[1]

After his victory at Second Manassas (Bull Run) in August 1862, Confederate General Robert E. Lee decided to move his Army of Northern Virginia out of war-torn Virginia and invade the North for the first time. Lee's troops (about 40,000 men) began crossing the Potomac River into Maryland on September 4, 1862, and headed toward Frederick. Lee intended to push on into Pennsylvania, but his supply and communication lines stretched back into Virginia and were threatened when a 13,000-man Union garrison remained in place at Harpers Ferry (now part of West Virginia). Against the advice of Maj. Gen. James Longstreet, Lee divided his exhausted army into several pieces. About half of it moved under Maj. Gen. Thomas J. "Stonewall" Jackson to surround and capture Harpers Ferry from

---

1 Please see the Appendix, "Antietam's Dunker Church: A Tactical Overview," by former Antietam National Battlefield historian Ted Alexander for more detail on the specific fighting in the area of the Dunker Church.

Gen. Robert E. Lee. LOC

several different directions. Much of the balance remained west of South Mountain, with some of Longstreet's command pushing on to Hagerstown, Maryland, near the Pennsylvania line. Troops under Maj. Gen. Daniel H. Hill moved onto the mountain itself to hold the main gaps that sliced through it.

After the Union debacle at Second Bull Run at the end of August, President Lincoln put Maj. Gen. George McClellan in command to organize and prepare the Army of the Potomac in and around Washington, D.C.

The general worked fast and the army was ready to fight much sooner than Lee had anticipated. In early September, McClellan began moving westward in several columns toward South Mountain, protecting the capital as he moved while seeking to determine Lee's whereabouts. The Union army reached Frederick on September 12 just as the last of Lee's Confederates were leaving town. On the 13th, a Union soldier found a copy of Lee's Special Order 191. The

Maj. Gen. George B. McClellan. LOC

"Lost Order," as it became known, detailed Lee's plan of operations for the campaign. Realizing his enemy was divided, McClellan moved quickly to capitalize on his good fortune. He struck the Confederates holding the passes on South Mountain on September 14, forcing Hill to vacate Crampton's, Fox's, and Turner's gaps that evening in a stunning tactical defeat of part of Lee's army. That desperate news, coupled with the Harpers Ferry problem, prompted Lee to move the bulk of his command to the heights around Sharpsburg in preparation for abandoning his campaign and retreating back over the Potomac River. When word arrived on the 15th that the entire Union garrison had surrendered at Harpers Ferry, Lee decided to concentrate his forces at Sharpsburg and and continue the campaign.

The century-old small farming community had grown along Antietam Creek, a meandering scenic stream fordable at many points and spanned by several stone bridges.[2] Lee positioned his troops along a series of ridges and hills west of the creek. His center and right were commanded by Longstreet, while his left was under Jackson. About one mile behind the Confederate lines was Blackford's (Pack Horse) Ford on the Potomac—the only escape route for Lee's army back into Virginia.

On September 15 and 16, General McClellan's army arrived east of Antietam Creek. As the Union plan developed, McClellan intended to cross the creek and strike Lee's exposed left flank (Jackson) early on the morning of September 17, followed by strikes against his center. Another large part of his army would cross on the Union left and move directly against Sharpsburg, which was essentially Lee's right flank.

The Mumma Church was just southeast of the West Woods next to the Hagerstown Pike. The small whitewashed building on its little rocky plateau stood out brightly against the dark backdrop of the woods and would become the focal point of three major Union attacks during the morning phase of the battle. Jackson's men, together with reinforcements under Maj. Gen. John Bell Hood, were deployed in and around the Dunker Church in the West Woods and northward on the left flank of Lee's army. Their location there, together with McClellan's battle plan, placed the church in the center of the fighting—a distinctive landmark upon which the Union troops guided while maneuvering through the smoke, noise, and bloody confusion of battle. The

---

2   The Union named most of the battles after natural features (Antietam Creek), while the South tended to name battles after the nearest city or town (Sharpsburg).

Maj. Gen. Thomas J. "Stonewall" Jackson. *LOC*

Mumma Church became something akin to a lighthouse shining brightly through a raging storm at sea.[3]

After some preliminary fighting on the evening of the 16th, the main battle kicked off in earnest about dawn on September 17 when Gen. Joseph Hooker's First Corps fell heavily against Jackson's left. The initial attack was followed with more assaults by Maj. Gen. Joseph Mansfield's Twelfth Corps, and later, Maj. Gen. Edwin Sumner's Second Corps, which reached the area of the Dunker Church. Some of the fiercest fighting of the entire war raged in D. R. Miller's cornfield, the East Woods, and the West Woods, all of which surrounded the small white church. Unfortunately for McClellan, his attacks were delivered as a series uncoordinated punches, each powerful in its own right, but none of sufficient weight to fatally crack the Confederate line. Southern troops fought magnificently, shifting from place to place to fill gaps in the line. Reinforcements from Longstreet's center and right shuttled northward to help bolster Jackson's sagging front.

Col. Stephen D. Lee's Confederate artillery battalion of four batteries (19 guns) lined the ridge across Hagerstown Pike from the Dunker Church. His artillerists did their best to fight off the distant Union artillery pieces as

---

3 "The Dunkard Church," Antietam National Battlefield Site; Ted Alexander, *The Battle of Antietam: The Bloodiest Day* (Charleston, SC, 2011). The Mumma Church was simply in the wrong place at the wrong time because it was where Lee and Jackson decided to make a defensive stand. The site encompassed what co-author Alann Schmidt calls "the three Rs"—the ridge for high ground advantage, the road for mobility, and the river behind it, limiting the ability to maneuver and thus forcing any flanking operation to fall upon that general location.

well as attacking Union infantry. The Southern guns were mostly of smaller weight, however, and badly outgunned by the Union pieces. Of Colonel Lee's 300 men, 86 fell killed or wounded, and 60 horses were lost. The dead Confederates depicted in Alexander Gardner's famous, though horrific, images of the Dunker Church area taken just two days after the battle were mostly artillerymen from Captain William W. Parker's (Richmond) Virginia Battery of S. D. Lee's battalion.

By late morning the combat had shifted from Lee's left to his center. There, a three-hour fight broke out along a sunken farm lane (forever after known as the Sunken Road or Bloody Lane), within sight of the Dunker Church. The carnage on both sides was nearly indescribable. According to General Longstreet, soldiers were "mowed down like grass before the scythe," their bodies lying in heaps. The Union attacks finally broke through at the Bloody Lane. Lee's entire army was in danger of disintegrating. Only stout defensive artillery work, knots of brave infantry standing firm, and a failure of the Union commanders to renew the attack, saved the Army of Northern Virginia from a catastrophic defeat.[4]

Once the line stablized in the center the serious fighting shifted in earnest to Lee's right flank. Initial combat there began as early as 10:00 a.m. when Maj. Gen. Ambrose Burnside's Ninth Corps began assaulting the Lower Bridge over the Antietam—the most contested of the three bridges (Upper, Middle, and Lower). The bluffs overlooking what became known as "Burnside Bridge" were held that morning by 550 Georgians under Brig. Gen. Robert Toombs, who slaughtered the attackers as they funneled themselves across the narrow span. About 1:00 p.m., however, low on ammunition and heavily outnumbered, Toombs' men were finally driven from their positions after Union forces forced their way across.

Once across, Burnside massed his forces on the western bank of Antietam Creek and prepared for an all-out assault against Lee's right, which had been stripped of men and guns to support his previously embattled left and center. Burnside's men were driving ahead with little to stop them when Maj. Gen. A. P. Hill's "Light Division," after a 17-mile forced march from Harpers Ferry, arrived on the battlefield just when and where it was needed. Hill fed his brigades into the fight and repulsed Burnside.

4 Ronald H. Bailey, ed., *The Bloodiest Day: The Battle of Antietam* (Alexandria, VA, 1984), 119.

Painting by Captain James Hope of the early morning Union advance on the Dunker Church and West Woods. Confederate Colonel Stephen D. Lee's artillery battalion is in the foreground. Many of the Southern artillery pieces were small caliber iron guns, and the ammunition was often unreliable, causing some to refer to the experience as "Artillery Hell." *ANB*

The 12-hour, nearly nonstop battle, finally ended about 6:00 p.m. Because of the lateness of the hour and the presence of only a single ford, it was impossible for General Lee to safely withdraw his thousands of wounded, artillery, wagons, and men safely across the Potomac by dawn. The Confederate leader consolidated his lines, had ammunition distributed, and ordered that as many wounded as possible be collected and sent south of the river in preparation to repel additional Union attacks expected the following day. When McClellan declined the opportunity to attack, Lee began withdrawing his battered army on the evening of Thursday, September 18. General McClellan held the battlefield, but was convinced that his Army of the Potomac had been too roughly handled to advance and take advantage of Lee's precarious retreat. A bloody rear guard action at

Shepherdstown on September 19 blunted a tepid Union pursuit. Lee's first invasion of the North was officially over.[5]

The size of Lee's army at Sharpsburg on September 17 is still vigorously debated, but there is no doubt nearly all of his men were engaged in the fighting. Of his approximately 87,000 troops on the field, McClellan committed only some 50,000 men to the battle itself, holding a large portion of his army in reserve. Thousands of Federals never fired a shot. Some 23,000 Americans were killed, wounded, or captured in this single day of combat—the bloodiest day in American history.[6]

---

5 "Antietam," Antietam National Battlefield, Maryland (National Park Service, U. S. Department of the Interior, 2009). Automobiles were allowed to cross "Burnside Bridge" (the Lower Bridge) until as late as 1964; Pack Horse Ford, Blackford's Ford, Boteler's Ford, and Shepherdstown Ford, are all names for essentially the same ford on the Potomac River.

6 Stephen W. Sears, *Landscape Turned Red: The Battle of Antietam* (New Haven and New York, 1983), 296. Some 50,000 men fell killed or wounded at Gettysburg during Lee's second invasion of the North in early July 1863, but over three days of battle, not one.

Confederate dead, mostly from Parker's Virginia battery of Stephen D. Lee's artillery battalion, in front of the Dunker Church as photographed by Alexander Gardner just two days after the battle. LOC

Clara Barton, the "Angel of the Battlefield" and later founder of the American Red Cross, traveled to the battlefield with a wagon full of bandages and other medical supplies. She helped thousands of dying and wounded soldiers on both sides, nearly all of whom were being cared for in scores of impromptu field hospitals.[7]

If there was ever any real chance that Great Britain and France would intervene on the side of the Confederacy, Lee's retreat back into Virginia ended that hope. On September 22, 1862, President Abraham Lincoln used the strategic victory to issue his preliminary Emancipation Proclamation declaring all slaves held in the rebellious states free as of January 1, 1863. For Mr. Lincoln, the war now had a dual purpose: defeating the Confederacy to bring the states in rebellion back into the Union as soon as possible, and to

7   See, generally, Stephen Krensky, *Clara Barton* (New York, 2011).

end slavery once and for all throughout the reunited Union. England and France, which had already banned slavery, could no longer take up the Confederate cause.

Lincoln visited the recovering Army of the Potomac in and around Sharpsburg from October 1-4, 1862, and soon thereafter removed General McClellan from command. The general, he complained, had "the slows" and the president (and others) believed he should have capitalized on Lee's retreat and aggressively followed up and defeated him. General Ambrose Burnside was promoted to lead the army.[8]

8 Stephen W. Sears, *George B. McClellan: The Young Napoleon* (New York, 1988), 330-31, 338; Sears, *Landscape Turned Red: The Battle of Antietam*, 336-340.

Chapter 5

September Mourn

*R*en. Freeman Ankrum of The Brethren Church, a noted Brethren historian, liked to wax poetic in his writings. Here is his description of Sunday, September 14, 1862, of the Antietam or Cumberland Valley:

> There was a haze over the distant mountain off to the east. The corn was ripening in the autumn sun. The leaves of the oaks and the maples in the nearby grove indicated the change of the season. The Cumberland Valley, always beautiful but never more so than in the lazy, hazy days of September and the following colorful days of October, lay bathed in beauty.[1]

That Sabbath morning Brethren Elder David Long and Daniel Wolf (a minister but not yet an elder) preached to the little flock in the Mumma Church. Elder Long, then forty-two but still in his prime, read and preached from the Psalms.

It would have been just another Sunday worship service, but this day was different. Everyone knew there were great armies, North and South, marching in their midst, and the conversation was fraught with fear for the

---

1 Ankrum, *Sidelights on Brethren History*, 109.

Brethren Elder David Long of the Manor Church near Tilghmanton, MD. *BHLA*

coming days. These concerns were realized later in the afternoon when a distant cannonade from the fighting at South Mountain, about seven miles to the east, reverberated across the valley and clouds of battle smoke drifted over the high mountain passes.

At some point, a cannonball reportedly pierced the east wall of the Long house. *Terry Barkley*

Following the worship service, the nervous members of the small congregation slowly made their way back to their farms, or to have a lunch with family and friends at their farms. As was their custom, Samuel and Elizabeth Mumma invited guests to enjoy a noonday meal with them at their home just east of the small white church.

Later that same afternoon, children playing outside at the Mumma farm reported to the adults that they saw smoke hovering over South Mountain; the battle there had just begun. Also that afternoon, more than 100 people made their way to the home of Elder David Long a couple miles west of the Manor Church near the village of Tilghmanton (but closer to Fairplay). Their apprehensions and concerns were justified. Still, even the David and

Mary (Reichard) Long home was in range of the converging armies. Troops would cross the farm, trampling its crops and doing other damage, but the house itself would be generally left alone. At some point, a cannonball reportedly pierced the east wall of the house.[2]

Elder David Long, the father of twelve children, eleven of whom lived to maturity, liked to say that "the gospel is free." Dunker elders, nearly all farmers, served for life without pay in the plural free-ministry of the Brethren. Of Elder Long's children, six daughters and five sons, three daughters married Dunker ministers, and four of the five sons became Dunker ministers.[3]

Austin Cooper, the Church of the Brethren minister and historian who was at the forefront of trying to get the Dunker Church reconstructed on the Antietam battlefield, was convinced that during the two days before the battle, while forming his lines on what would become the left flank of General Lee's army, "Stonewall" Jackson had used the Dunker Church as his headquarters. Cooper, who was writing a book about the Dunker Church with the working title *Antietam Dunkard Church*, interviewed locals familiar with the Mumma Church and the battle. These included veterans of the fighting, North and South, and informed historians of the church and the battle like O. T. Reilly, the battlefield's first tour guide, Fred Cross, E. Russell Hicks, Leon Carnahan, Richard Leatherman, Page T. Otto, and Fred Peterman.

During the early part of the engagement, General Jackson used the little Dunker Church for his headquarters. From this prominent place he had the advantage of enjoying a wide panorama of the sprawling, undulating fields, a viewshed that apparently included the headquarters of General McClellan,

---

2 Ibid., 109-112. Ted Alexander, retired historian at Antietam National Battlefield, believes it is quite possible the damage to the David Long house and farm came about not in 1862, but during General Lee's second invasion of the North in 1863, when Union and Confederate troops passed through the general area a second time on their way to Gettysburg. Rev. Ankrum believed the damage was inflicted during the Maryland Campaign/Antietam. Further evidence on this issue is presented in Chapter Eight. Rev. McKinley Coffman, the grandnephew of Elder David Long, may have given the last sermon preached in the Dunker Church before it was blown down in a windstorm in 1921. Newton L. Poling, "The Dunkers: Their Customs and Life Style in the Antietam Valley," a paper delivered by Rev. Poling at the 1992 Antietam Volunteer Seminar in Hagerstown, MD, March 21, 1992.

3 Ankrum, *Sidelights on Brethren History*, 112-114.

who had secured the comfortable dwelling of Philip Pry on the north bank of Antietam Creek well up a limestone outcropping hill.[4]

Rev. Cooper, the pastor of the Sharpsburg Church of the Brethren from 1945-1947, regularly spoke with the locals about the Dunker Church and the Antietam battle itself. Philip Lum, an eyewitness to the battle, told Cooper that

> . . . about midmorning a group of Confederate snipers were in the church shooting out of the doors and windows. One was up on top of the church shooting at Union troops out of the small [attic] windows. He related that General Stonewall Jackson rode near the church and heard the shooting. On investigating the cause [he] found the men in the church. He immediately ordered them out and sent them out into the thickest of the battle far down the line...

Lum praised Jackson's "great respect for the House of the Lord." If General Jackson did make the Mumma Church his headquarters before the battle commenced, he did not sleep there. On the night of September 16, Jackson, who had had little rest of any kind for two days, spotted a tree with roots running along top of the ground. He used one of the roots for a pillow and fell fast asleep.[5]

While at the Dunker Church later on the day of the battle, Jackson supposedly detailed five couriers to deliver a message to General A. P. Hill, who was en route to the battlefield from Harpers Ferry with his "Light Division." Hill was approaching the Confederate right from Blackford's Ford on the Potomac River after a harrowing 17-mile forced march. Of the

4 Rev. Austin Cooper, "Antietam Battlefield Landmark to be Reconstructed," in *Antietam Dunkard Church*, 2. It was recently concluded the Pry House was more McClellan's command post than his headquarters. New evidence places McClellan's headquarters from September 16-20 in Keedysville, northeast of Sharpsburg. The headquarters site was likely south of the cemetery in Keedysville along both sides of the road leading to the Upper Bridge over Antietam Creek. See Thomas G. Clemens, "In Search of McClellan's Headquarters," *Civil War Times* (June 2016), 26-33; See also Ezra A. Carman (Thomas G. Clemens, ed.), *The Maryland Campaign of 1862*, vol. 2: *Antietam* (El Dorado Hills, CA, 2012).

5 Rev. Austin Cooper, "Upon This Rock—Build," 13, *Antietam Dunkard Church*; James I. Robertson, Jr., *Stonewall Jackson: The Man, The Soldier, The Legend* (New York, NY, 1997), 611.

A view of the damage on and around the Dunker Church, taken by Alexander Gardner within days after the end of the battle. *U. S. Army Heritage and Education Center, Carlisle Barracks, PA.*

five messengers Jackson dispatched, one was killed and two were wounded. The pair of riders who made it through to Hill found the general eating green corn from the cob. Before leaving Jackson at the church, one of the riders gave Stonewall a drink of milk from his canteen. The Rebel messenger had milked a cow in the woods behind the Dunker Church just a short time earlier.[6]

6 This story was told to O. T. Reilly by a group of Confederate veterans touring the battlefield in 1911. O. T. Reilly, "Stories of Antietam," in *The Battlefield of Antietam* (Sharpsburg, MD: O. T. Reilly, 1906), np.

Some 12,000 men fell killed and wounded in just over three hours (roughly one man per second) during the morning phase of the battle.[7] Ironically, in the middle of this whirlwind of violence stood the small whitewashed building founded on the principles of peace and dedicated to the brotherhood of all men. Nearly every commander who fought in that area of the battlefield mentioned the church in his after-action report. Some referred to it as a schoolhouse. Confederate General Hood called it "St. Mumma's church," and a Confederate artillery officer referred to it as "the old Dutch Church."[8]

Horrific scenes permeated the area in and around the church. After carrying kettles of beans and buckets of water to soldiers in the field, some young Dunker boys found themselves on the rise at the Dunker Church. There, they found the body of a young Confederate drummer boy about their own age propped against a large oak tree not far from the church itself. His hat was pulled down over his face as if he were asleep. His intact drum and drumsticks lay near him. In one hand he held a short worn pencil and in the other a scrap of paper on which he had been writing. It soon became obvious that he was scribbling a hurried note to his mother:

Dear Mother I am here beside a little white church. I have been wounded in the leg. It don't hurt much just sore. I'm all right and will be home before long. When all this . . .

And there the note abruptly ended. When one of the boys looked under the young Rebel's hat, he found himself staring into the glazed eyes of the dead boy. It was only then that he realized part of the back of his head had been shot away.

Later, Captain John A. Tompkins and men of Company (Battery) A, First Rhode Island Light Artillery, also came across the dead Confederate drummer boy. The Union artillerists carefully "pulled his hat back down

---

7 A full tactical account of the fighting in this area is found in the Appendix "Antietam's Dunker Church: A Tactical Overview," by Ted Alexander.

8 Schmidt, Draft, *Historic American Buildings Survey, Dunker Church, Antietam National Battlefield*; Carol Reardon and Tom Vossler, *A Field Guide to Antietam: Experiencing the Battlefield Through Its History, Places, and People* (Chapel Hill, NC, 2016), 129, 326. Confederate General John Bell Hood used a map that listed "S. Mumma" as the property owner.

over his face . . . took the unfinished note to his mother and stuck it down in his shirt pocket and left him there." The unnamed Confederate lad became known as the "drummer boy of Dunker Church."[9]

Another sad story—just one among thousands that day—relates a wounded young Union soldier who had sought refuge and medical care inside the church. He was sitting beside a window with his arm on the window still and his head resting on his arm when a bullet fired from a Confederate sharpshooter in a tree in the West Woods struck him in the side of his head. The force jerked him to his feet before his lifeless body fell out of the window onto the ground.[10]

A further unsettling account tells of a Confederate soldier dragging a wounded Union officer inside the church to more safely steal his boots. The officer resisted the theft, yelling "Go away out of that, you son of a witch!" The Rebel pulled a pistol, aimed it at the officer, and "blew his brains out." The account was published in a Cincinnati newspaper in September 1867. Veterans of the battle, including the Confederate who pulled the trigger, visited the battlefield five years later. The veteran who told the journalist the story seemed unruffled by the murder: "We all know that about Jim. But we can't hold men to account for murdering in war. Not much! His note is good in the bank any day. He's one of our best farmers."[11]

William "Bill" Bussard, apparently another witness to the battle, told Rev. Cooper that the Dunker Church was initially used by the Confederates as a first aid station:

> A white 'flag of truce' was hoisted ontop the little church to denote it as a hospital. Soldiers were placed on the pews. Later so many were brought there that the pews were taken out in the yard and placed under the great oak trees and straw was placed on the floor and soldiers of both sides were

9 John P. Smith, a local Sharpsburg school teacher, wrote the article in *The Morning Herald*, Hagerstown, MD (January 28, 1951); interview with Fred Peterman, 1962, by Rev. Austin Cooper. Captain Tompkins's son, Dr. John A. Tompkins of Baltimore, Maryland, told this story to Rev. Cooper. Cooper, *Antietam Dunkard Church*, a 14- page set of notes in outline form presented to the Hagerstown Civil War Round Table, January 26, 1967, page 8, Austin Cooper Collection, BHLA, Elgin, IL.

10 Cooper, "Killed Through the Church Window," *Antietam Dunkard Church*.

11 *Cincinnati Daily Gazette*, September 21, 1867; Reardon and Vossler, *A Field Guide to Antietam*, 130, 326.

Clara Barton, the "Angel of the Battlefield," founded the American Red Cross. *LOC*

laid on the floor. Those pews in the yard contained wounded soldiers also. The pulpit [preachers' table] was the plain, long, sturdy table that was used by the elders and [also] known as 'The Elders table.' Men were operated on from this table and it was used to bear the wounded for the amputation of arms and legs. Mr. Lumm told this author [Cooper] that he remembered the next day after the battle seeing piles of arms and legs piled outside the [north] windows facing West Wood, high as the window sills. Mr. Fred Peter[man] said that his father, James Peterman, and Samuel Mumma, Sr., and John Ecker, took wheel barrow loads of arms and legs out and buried them alongside West Wood. Blood laid [lay] thick and hard all over the floor and pews and furniture for weeks. They decided to just let things as they were so that the rain could wash them clean.[12]

As soon as they were allowed to return to their battle-scarred meetinghouse, the Dunkers arrived to help take care of the wounded. They moved all who could safely be evacuated to the Poffenberger hospital, where Clara Barton had opened her two hospitals on the Poffenberger and Middlekauf farms. Those who were very ill and/or wounded were taken back to the old Daniel Miller Meetinghouse (the home where the Mumma congregation first worshipped]. Like so many other buildings, it had also been turned in a medical facility (Franklin Hospital). Many of these men had pneumonia and some were suffering from typhoid fever. Most of them were

12 Cooper, "Upon This Rock—Build," 13.

taken into the homes of the Dunkers. Some remained there that fall and even through the winter months.[13]

Rev. Cooper claimed both the Joseph and Samuel Poffenberger farms were used by Clara Barton. "She set up her hospitals first in the Joseph Poffenberger buildings, John Middlekauff house, the Dunbar Mill, the Samuel Poffenberger barn, Michael Miller house, the Daniel Miller House and barn," he wrote.[14]

Henry Neikirk was a member of the Mumma Church who also sat on the original building committee for the little building. He would later serve as the foreman for the committee repairing and rebuilding the church after the battle. Neikirk lived on the east side of the battlefield and his home became an important hospital once the fighting stoppped. On September 15, just two days before the battle began, five Confederate soldiers looking for horses accosted Neikirk near his home. It is possible that Southern sympathizers in the area had informed the Rebels that Neikirk had many fine horses. Neikirk was warned about the approaching "strangers" and had his sons take his eleven horses away and hide them.

When the Rebels questioned him, Neikirk refused to tell them where he had moved his horses. The infuriated Southerners, wrote Rev. Cooper,

> took the reigns [reins] of Henry's horse, took the straps, tied them around his feet and tied them to the limb of a large white oak tree. This left poor Henry dangling, head down, along the creek. The men (soldiers) went to the Neikirk home, demanded food from the women, searched the house. . . . By this time it was dark. . . . They then rode off with his saddle horse, headed toward the Mumma house. It was late that night that the sons returned down the creek walking. . . . They heard the feeble cries of their father calling for help. They cut him down in time to save his life. . . . He was unconscious most of the night . . . but recovered . . .[15]

---

13 Ibid., 13. The piece only says "Poffenberger" farm and hospital, and does not specify whether it was the Joseph or Samuel Poffenberger farm. It was long thought that the Joseph Poffenberger farm was where Clara Barton opened one of her two hospitals, but it has now been proven by James Atkinson, former historian at Antietam National Battlefield, that it was on the Samuel Poffenberger farm. Schildt, *Drums Along the Antietam*, 195-196.

14 Cooper, *Antietam Dunkard Church*.

15 Cooper, "Hanging of Henry Neikirk," *Antietam Dunkard Church*.

A drawing of the burning of the Samuel Mumma farm at Antietam on September 17, 1862, by Alfred Waud. *LOC*

Ironically, the only farm on the battlefield deliberately marked for destruction by the Confederates was the house, barn, and outbuildings of Dunker pacifists, Samuel and Elizabeth Mumma. Samuel's first wife had died, and Elizabeth was his second wife. Together the two marriages had produced sixteen children, ten of whom were at home when the battle began.[16]

The Mumma farm sat right in front of the Confederate lines north of Sharpsburg, and officers worried that Union soldiers would use the house and buildings as sharpshooter nests. Sergeant Major James F. Clark of the 3rd North Carolina, part of Brig. Gen. Roswell S. Ripley's brigade (D. H. Hill's division), was dispatched with a half-dozen enlisted men to burn the house. The only one of the party injured was Sergeant Major Clark, who was nursed by an unidentified woman in a Confederate hospital behind the lines. Her identity haunted him. Long after the war in the early 1900s, Clark wrote

16 Elizabeth was the daughter of devout Brethren Daniel and Catherine Funk Miller.

A view of the burned Samuel Mumma house and its surrounding farm buildings, taken by Alexander Gardner days after the September 17th battle. LOC

a letter in which he described "a woman young and beautiful and black-haired" who helped bandage his arm." He admitted he "often wondered if she was any of the family and where they went when caught between the lines of battle."[17]

Samuel Mumma, Jr. replied to Clark's letter on March 22, 1906. In it, he explained that the house, "a large brick colonial one, near the Dunker Church," had belonged to his father, Samuel, Sr. He informed Clark that the family, fearing the worst as the armies massed nearby, had left their home with little more than the clothes on their backs on the afternoon of Monday, September 15, bound for the Manor Church near Tilghmanton four miles

17 James F Clark, Letter, March 19, 1906, from New Bern, NC, to "Postmaster, Sharpsburg, Maryland." Samuel Mumma, Jr, Letter, March 22, 1906, shared by Mumma's granddaughter Virginia Mumma Hildebrand. Schildt, *Drums Along the Antietam*, 184-185; Walker and Kirkman, "Samuel Mumma Farm," 52-61; Poling, "The Dunkers: Their Customs and Life Style in the Antietam Valley," March 21, 1992.

away where many of the Brethren took refuge from the coming battle. The younger Samuel returned with a friend to his home to get some clothing on Tuesday, September 16, "but found that everything of value had been taken." The family had always thought their home had been shelled and burned by cannon fire from a Union battery belonging to Gen. Israel B. Richardson's command. "Our family then went to a friend's house [Sherrick's] until spring," continued Mumma's letter. "In the spring of 1863 we rebuilt our house and had just moved in a few weeks before the Armies [Union and Confederate] went to Gettysburg."

When the Confederates were passing through Sharpsburg once again, Samuel Mumma, Jr., was approached by a Confederate officer who claimed that he and "eight other men" had been detailed by General Ripley to burn the Mumma house. His description to the younger Mumma of the house and its contents solidified his claim. "We lost crops, fencing and everything," lamented Mumma in his reply in 1906, "all amounting to from $8,000.00 to $10,000.00 and were never recompensed as the Government claimed it was damaged by being right in the heart of the battle."

Mumma closed his letter by addressing the identity of the girl who had treated the wounded Sergeant Clark. The former Confederate had likely been treated at the home of Harry Reel, southwest of the Dunker Church, explained Mumma, which was the "nearest hospital that I knew of." Harry Reel had a daughter with black hair, but "she is now dead and the rest of the family have moved west."[18]

Henry Kyd Douglas was from "Ferry Hill," just across the Potomac River from Shepherdstown and only about three miles from the battlefield. Douglas was the youngest member of Stonewall Jackson's staff and one of the general's favorites. About midnight on the evening of September 17-18, he recorded what he saw near the Dunker Church:

> On my way to [General Jubal A.] Early I went off the pike and was compelled to go through a field in the rear of Dunker Church, over which, to and fro, the pendulum of battle had swung several times that day. It was a dreadful scene, a veritable field of blood. The dead and dying lay as thick over it as harvest sheaves. The pitiable cries for water and appeals for help were much more horrible to listen to than the deadliest sounds of battle.

18 Mumma, Letter, March 22, 1906; Walker and Kirkman, "Samuel Mumma Farm," 52-61.

Silent were the dead, and motionless. But here and there were raised stiffened arms; heads made a last effort to lift themselves from the ground; prayers were mingled with oaths, the oaths of delirium; men were wriggling over the earth; and midnight hid all distinction between the blue and grey. My horse trembled under me in terror, looking down at the ground, sniffing the scent of blood, stepping falteringly as a horse will over or by the side of human flesh; afraid to stand still, hesitating to go on, his animal instinct shuddering at this cruel human mystery. Once his foot slid into a little shallow filled with blood and spurted a little stream on his legs and my boots. I had a surfeit of blood that day and I couldn't stand this. I dismounted and giving the reins to my courier I started on foot into the wood of Dunker Church.[19]

Scores of dead and dying horses added to the human carnage littering the battlefield. One gun battery near the Dunker Church lost twenty-six horses. Samuel Mumma hauled fifty-five dead horses from his farm alone, dragging them to the East Woods where they were later burned.[20]

An Ohio soldier who stopped by the battered Dunker Church just after the heavy fighting subsided took the time to record the following scene, which may attest to the claim that the church grounds also served as a temporary cemetery:

A little crowd of soldiers were standing about it, and within, a few severely wounded rebels were stretched on the benches, one of whom was raving in his agony. Surgical aid and proper attendance had already been furnished, and we did not join the throng of curious visitors within. Out in the grove behind the little church the dead had already been collected in groups ready for burial, some of them wearing our uniform, but the large majority dressed in gray. No matter in what direction we turned, it was all the same shocking picture, awakening awe rather than pity, benumbing the senses

19 Henry Kyd Douglas, *I Rode With Stonewall* (Chapel Hill, 1940, 1961), 172-173; Barkley, "Antietam, Battle of," 41.

20 Ankrum, *Sidelights on Brethren History*, 105; Schildt, *Drums Along the Antietam*, 289.

The rebuilt Samuel Mumma farm house and buildings as they appear today on the Antietam National Battlefield. *LOC*

rather than touching the heart, glazing the eye with horror rather than filling it with tears.[21]

On September 18 a truce was called between the two sides near the church to exchange wounded and bury the dead. Men who just hours earlier had been desperately trying to kill one another came together for the common good beneath the white flag. The scene was recorded by renowned Civil War artist Alfred R. Waud who, like the soldiers themselves, must have sensed the irony of it all. "It was paradoxical. "Bewildering. Yet, strangely fascinating," admitted Ronald J. Gordon of the Church of the Brethren. "The previous day they fiercely struggled to kill each other on these very grounds, and now before Waud's pencil they corporately mused over the hideous import of their actions."

Martin E. Snavely was one of the locals hired to haul coffins to the railroad station in Hagerstown to be shipped home. He drove a six-horse

21 George F. Noyes, *The Bivouac and the Battlefield; or, Campaign Sketches in Virginia and Maryland* (New York, 1863), 216-217; see Reardon and Vossler, *A Field Guide to Antietam*, 130, 326.

Alfred Waud's "Flag of truce," when Union and Confederates gathered to recover the wounded and the dead near the Dunker Church on the day after the battle. LOC

team and picked up most of the caskets at the Dunker Church, which, after serving as a hospital, now served as an embalming station and morgue. Snavely remembered seeing a pile of arms and legs several feet high near one window on the north side of the church where an operating table was busy at work. A veteran of the battle claimed he was detailed to burn or bury the pile of arms and legs at the Dunker Church, something he would have done in or near the West Woods.[22]

Following the battle, general officers of the Union army, including McClellan and Ambrose E. Burnside, together with their wives, billeted for a time in the home of Brethren Elder Eli Yourtee of the Brownsville church in Washington County. According to Yourtee family tradition, when Abraham Lincoln visited the army at Antietam in October, the president "had a bit of lunch with them" on Thursday, October 2, 1862.[23]

---

22 Ronald J. Gordon, "Peace is Witnessed" from "Little Dunker Church: A Silent Witness For Peace," Church of the Brethren Network, August 1988, last updated March 2013, www. cob-net.org/antietam/; Reilly, "Stories of Antietam"; Schildt, *Drums Along the Antietam*, 288-289; Ernst, *Too Afraid To Cry*, 160-161; Ankrum, *Sidelights on Brethren History*, 103.

23 John W. Schildt, *Four Days in October* (Chewsville, MD, 1982), 22; Henry, *History of the Church of the Brethren in Maryland*, 335-337; Barkley, "Antietam, Battle of," 41.

Chapter 6

Nothing Sacred:
The Mumma Bible is Taken

For days following the battle, McClellan's Army of the Potomac was engaged in burying the dead and caring for the wounded of both sides. Large numbers of family members appeared, pouring over the horrific battlefield and combing the hospitals and temporary burial grounds in search of loved ones.

On September 28, eleven days after the Battle of Antietam ended, a Union corporal named Nathan F. Dykeman visited the heavily damaged Dunker Church. Dykeman served in Company H of 107th New York. Perhaps he was there to find a friend, or perhaps it was simple curiosity that drew him there. The whitewashed building was still being used as a hospital, and, as noted earlier, an embalming station and likely a cemetery. The altar Bible was there, back in its proper place and open on the preachers' [Elder's] table.

The scene that greeted the Union soldier was certainly poignant and surely one he never forgot. The table and bench pews had been impressed into service to attend to the scores of wounded and dying men being shuttled into and out of the building. The table was used for bloody operations, the pews reserved for men to lie upon while awaiting the surgeon's saw. By this time, most or all of the furniture would have been heavily stained with blood. What passed through Dykeman's mind at that moment will never be known,

An image of the Dunker Church, attributed to Alexander Gardner, taken soon after the end of the Civil War. Note that the heavy damage sustained by the building during the Battle of Antietam has been repaired. LOC

but the Union corporal decided to take the church's Bible with him as a battlefield souvenir. In the devastation and human carnage that is war, little or nothing remains sacred—not even the altar Bible of the Dunker Church. A comrade in Corporal Dykeman's regiment who was traveling home on a short furlough took the heavy leather-bound book (which measured 9 x 11 x 2 1/2 inches) to Dykeman's home in Millport, New York, for safe-keeping.[1]

Nathan F. Dykeman had mustered in as a corporal at Havana (now the town of Montour Falls), New York, on July 25, 1862. He was 24 years old when he joined the Union army. His brother James, who was 22,

1   An article in *Inglenook* dated May 1, 1906, claimed that this Bible had been "well put up" by the Brethren, as quoted in *The Gospel Messenger,* September 1, 1906. Both *Inglenook* and *The Gospel Messenger* are Brethren-related; Clem, "Civil War Footsteps: Black Farmer Plays Key Role in Return of Dunkard Bible," *Maryland Cracker Barrel* (December/January 2004) 10, 12, 14; Ankrum, *Sidelights on Brethren History*, 117-118; Henry, *History of the Church of the Brethren in Maryland*, 372-377.

accompanied him into the unit as a private. Together, the two young Schuyler County men served in the 107th New York Infantry in several of the war's bloodiest battles, including Antietam, Fredericksburg, Chancellorsville, and Gettysburg.

The 107th New York was transferred to south central Tennessee in early 1864, where it became part of the veteran Army of the Cumberland. James Dykeman participated in the Atlanta Campaign and was wounded at New Hope Church on May 25, 1864. He recuperated enough to rejoin his brother Nathan and the 107th New York to participate in William T. Sherman's occupation of Atlanta, its burning, and then the "March to the Sea" all the way to Savannah late that year.

The 107th New York was in Raleigh, North Carolina, when the war ended, and the regiment was ordered to return north to Bladensburg, Maryland, on the outskirts of Washington, D.C. The New Yorkers participated with Sherman's Western Army and thousands of other men in the Grand Review down Pennsylvania Avenue on May 24, 1865. Supposedly, this was the last time the Dykeman brothers, Nathan and James, marched together.

On May 29, 1865, while waiting to be mustered out of service, Nathan, James, and a comrade were walking to the Bladensburg Railroad Station along a double set of tracks. When they spotted a train coming toward them, the three men stepped off the tracks. Nathan, however, stepped onto an adjacent track. Perhaps the loud noise of the oncoming train's whistle meshed with that of a train coming up from behind the unsuspecting soldier. Nathan Dykeman was hit and killed instantly. "The Lord works in mysterious ways, His wonders to perform."[2]

Most authors and researchers assumed that Nathan Dykeman died around 1903 in Elmira, New York. However, the evidence does not support this conclusion and in fact he died in Bladensburg. Dykeman had been promoted to sergeant on December 1, 1863, and appears to have been buried in an unmarked grave. If his remains were ever returned home to the Elmira-Millport area, no record of that event has come to light.

According to his service record, Nathan's brother James was mustered out of the 107th New York Infantry on May 13, 1865, at Elmira, New York.

2   From the first two lines of a hymn by William Cowper, "God Moves in Mysterious Ways," 1774.

This fact calls into question whether he had, in fact, marched with his brother in the Grand Review in Washington on May 24, 1865, and whether he was with Nathan when he was killed on May 29. James Dykeman died in 1884 in Peabody, Kansas.[3]

3   One course stated that Nathan Dykeman was walking with "two other men." Lt. Colonel Newton T. Colby, *The Civil War Papers of Lt. Colonel Newton T. Colby, New York Infantry*, William E. Hughes, ed. (Jefferson, NC, 2003), 168; Military Service Records of Nathan F. and James F. Dykeman, Nicholas P. Picerno's Union Database, Bridgewater, VA; Clem, "Civil War Footsteps: Black Farmer Plays Key Role in Return of Dunkard Bible," 10, 12, 14. See also Richard Clem, "Travels and Travails of 'Battlefield Bible'," *The Washington Times*, June 18, 2004; Lori Lynn Sullivan, "A Battle, A Brown Bundle, and a Black Farmer," at https://lorilynnsullivan.com/tag/dunkard-bible/; "State and Nation Have Helped Veterans Adorn Picturesque Antietam Battlefield," *The Washington Post*, September 15, 1907, M8; Henry, *History of the Church of the Brethren in Maryland*, 372-377; Freeman Ankrum, "Antietam, Maryland, Dunker Bible," *The Brethren Evangelist* (November 17, 1951), 5-6, 10-11; See also Freeman Ankrum, "The Antietam Bible," *Gospel Messenger* (February 16, 1952), 10-12.

Chapter 7

John T. Lewis
and the "Antietam Bible"

The Holy Bible taken from the Dunker Church by Corporal Nathan F. Dykeman remained with his family until 1903. In the fall of that year, while the 107th New York Veterans Association was holding a reunion in Elmira, New York, a woman appeared with a Bible and a request for the men of Company H.

As it turned out, she was a sister of Nathan and James Dykeman, and the Bible was the same one stolen from the Dunker Church. She asked that it be returned to its rightful owners. The woman was described by one man as "afflicted" and in need of money. The aging veterans of Company H collected $10.00 for the book and agreed the Bible should be returned to the little church near Sharpsburg, Maryland. But how?

No one knew who to contact at the church or even if the church was still standing. All of them remembered how badly damaged the little Dunker meetinghouse was during the battle. Someone recalled there was a Dunker living close by, an old black man named John T. Lewis who worked for the Langdon family on the Quarry Farm in Elmira. When the former Union soldiers tracked him down and asked him, Lewis agreed to assist in returning the precious book to its rightful home.

Letters were exchanged with Elder John E. Otto of Sharpsburg, then pastor of the Dunker Church (and the last minister of that edifice). Elder Otto received the Bible by December 1903. He pasted the following on a separate sheet behind the front cover of the Bible:

John T. Lewis holding the "Antietam Bible" before it was shipped back to the Dunker Church in 1903. *BHLA*

Sharpsburg, December 4, 1903

The Bible was taken from the Church after the Battle of Antietam by Sergeant Nathan F. Dykeman, September 28, 1862, Regt. 107, Co. H, N.Y.S.V. [New York State Volunteers]. He is now dead, and it fell into the hands of his afflicted sister. She presented it to the Company [H] at their reunion this fall, 1903, for which they gave her ten dollars.

Their desire was to send it back to its home in the Brethren Church at Antietam Battlefield if it was still in existence. Through the kindness of Brother John T. Lewis, Elmira, N.Y., they received my name and address. They wrote me, I answered. The Bible is here after an absence of 41 years, 2 months, 6 days. It is supposed to have been placed in the Church by Daniel Miller.

John E. Otto[1]

Before the Bible was shipped express to Sharpsburg, John T. Lewis, who was then 68, was photographed holding the "lost Bible" of the Dunker Church, sometimes referred to as the "Antietam Bible."[2]

---

1 Elder Otto was the son-in-law of Daniel Miller, who was the great-grandfather of Ruth Otto of Sharpsburg. Daniel Miller died at the age of eighty-four, just two months after the Battle of Antietam. His death was attributed "to the excitement of the battle."

2 Henry, *History of the Church of the Brethren in Maryland*, 372; Ankrum, *Sidelights on Brethren History*, 117, 120-121; Ankrum, "The Antietam Bible," 10-12; Clem, "Civil War Footsteps: Black Farmer Plays Key Role in Return of Dunkard Bible," 12; Poling, "The Dunkers: Their Customs and Life Style in the Antietam Valley," np.

John T. Lewis's own story is quite remarkable and worth relating in detail. He was born on January 10, 1835, in Carroll County, Maryland. It is not clear whether he was born free, or was set free at a later date. In the fall of 1853, at the age of eighteen, he joined the German Baptist Brethren (Dunkers) at the Pipe Creek congregation at Union Bridge near New Windsor, Maryland, making him one of the very few black members of that sect. He was later baptized at the Meadow Branch meetinghouse in Westminster, Maryland, by Elder Philip Boyle. Following his baptism, Lewis went to the Beaver Dam church at Union Bridge by letter in 1856. With war clouds approaching in 1860, he moved to the Marsh Creek congregation of the Brethren near Gettysburg, Pennsylvania. With the war raging, he moved again in 1862 to New York—missing the three-day carnage of Gettysburg in early July 1863. John finally settled in Elmira by 1864, where he worked a small farm in the East Hill section and performed odd jobs.

On July 27, 1865, John married a southern woman named Mary A. Stover. Their only son, also named John, lived only five months, though a daughter named Susanna Alice (or Susan), survived both parents before dying in 1923. Mary Lewis died on June 20, 1894. John suffered from various ailments including a spinal injury that forced him to walk in a stooped position, and dropsy. He was lovingly cared for by his daughter and died in an ambulance on the way to the hospital on July 23, 1906, at the age of 71. John, Mary, and their children are buried in the family plot, Lot 89, Section 12, in Woodlawn Cemetery in Elmira. John T. Lewis' grave remained unmarked for nearly a century until the Brethren Historical Committee of the Church of the Brethren raised money to place a proper stone on his grave. The bronze plaque on a granite base simply says, "John T. Lewis, 1835-1906."[3]

Lewis worked as a coachman and his wife, Mary, was one of the African American female servants who worked for the Langdon family on the Quarry Farm just outside of Elmira. The Lewis farm was less than a mile past

---

3 Herbert A. Wisbey, Jr., "John T. Lewis, Mark Twain's Friend in Elmira," in *Mark Twain Society Bulletin* (January 1984), 4; John T. Lewis File, BHLA, Elgin, IL; Henry, *History of the Church of the Brethren in Maryland*, 372-377; Ankrum, *Sidelights on Brethren History*, 117-122.

Quarry Farm on East Hill.[4] During the summer of 1877, Samuel Langhorne Clemens, better known as Mark Twain, arrived for his annual visit with his in-laws, the Langdons at Quarry Farm. Twain had married Olivia Langdon in 1870. In 1876, he finished his bestselling novel *The Adventures of Tom Sawyer* at the farm.

As it turns out, Twain and John Lewis developed a warm, personal, and lasting friendship that began in August 1877, when Lewis saved the lives of Twain's sister-in-law, Ida, her young daughter, six-year-old Julia, and the daughter's nurse, Nora.

Ida—Mrs. Charles Langdon—was driving her carriage down a steep hill on the way back from visiting friends on East Hill near the Lewis farm when the horse pulling the carriage began running. The out-of-control carriage plunged down the hill to what looked to be certain disaster. Fortunately for all concerned, John was coming up the hill on his heavy farm wagon loaded with manure. Even though he did not know who was in the careening carriage, John pulled his wagon across the road, forming something of a "V" with a fence along the route, and jumped out. Steadying himself, the powerful farmer somehow managed to grab the terrified horse by the bridle and, running alongside, bring it to a complete halt just yards before the road took a sharp turn in front of a deep gully. If Lewis not been able to stop the horse when he did, he and the ladies would have been thrown into the ravine to certain injury or death. There was no doubt in anyone's mind that John had put himself in real danger, and that his heroism had prevented an almost certain tragedy.[5]

The Langdon family showed its appreciation in a number of ways, including money and a fine gold watch bearing the inscription: "John T. Lewis, who saved three lives at the deadly peril of his own, August 23, 1877. This in grateful remembrance from Mrs. Charles J. Langdon."[6]

Twain offered Lewis autographed copies of his books and a little more money. With his new-found bounty, John paid off his sixty-four acre farm. Best of all, Lewis and Twain became close friends for the rest of their lives.

---

4   Wisbey, Jr., "John T. Lewis, Mark Twain's Friend in Elmira," 1-5.

5   Ibid., 1; Clem, "Civil War Footsteps: Black Farmer Plays Key Role in Return of Dunkard Bible," 12.

6   Wisbey, Jr., "John T. Lewis, Mark Twain's Friend in Elmira," 1; Henry, *History of the Church of the Brethren in Maryland*, 375; Ankrum, *Sidelights on Brethren History*, 119.

(Above and left): Old friends, writer and satirist Mark Twain, and John T. Lewis, photographed together at Quarry Farm, Elmira, New York, in the summer of 1903 for the November issue of *Ladies' Home Journal*. *LOC and BHLA*

Twain not only visited with Lewis during his annual visits to Quarry Farm, but kept up with him through family correspondence and even arranged for Lewis to receive a small pension. Twain continually concerned himself with Lewis' financial needs. The two old friends were photographed together at Quarry Farm in the summer of 1903 for the November issue of *Ladies' Home Journal*. This was the last full summer Mark Twain spent at Quarry Farm.[7]

Writing in 1903, Mark Twain related that John T. Lewis was:

7   Wisbey, Jr., "John T. Lewis, Mark Twain's Friend in Elmira," 3; Ankrum, *Sidelights on Brethren History*, 119; Kermon Thomasson, "Mark Twain and His Dunker Friend," *Church of the Brethren Messenger* (October 1985), 19, 21.

a friend of mine these many years—thirty-four in fact. He was my father-in-law's coachman forty years ago; was many years a farmer of Quarry Farm, and is still a neighbor. I have not known an honester man nor a more respect-worthy one. Twenty-seven years ago, by the prompt and intelligent exercise of his courage, presence of mind and extraordinary strength, he saved the lives of relatives of mine, whom a runaway horse was hurrying to destruction. Naturally I hold him in high and grateful regard.[8]

Dunker John Lewis liked to read and he loved to debate theological questions. He and the Quarry Farm's cook, "Auntie" Mary Cord, a Methodist, often engaged in heated theological discussions—arguments, really—much to the delight and amusement of Mark Twain. "Lewis was very black," wrote the famous author of *Tom Sawyer* and *Huckleberry Finn*, and . . .

> Auntie Cord was a bright mulatto. Lewis' wife was several shades lighter. Whenever the discussion began it shaded off toward the color line and insult. Auntie Cord was a Methodist; Lewis was a Dunkard. Auntie Cord was ignorant and dogmatic; Lewis could read and was intelligent. Theology invariably led to personality, and eventually to epithets, crockery, geology, and victuals.[9]

Planning for his own imminent death in 1906, the aging hero asked Brethren Elder J. Kurtz Miller of the Brooklyn Church to preach at his funeral. However, Miller was in Iowa when the time came and a replacement Brethren minister did not reach Elmira in time to oversee the sad event. The undertaker for Elmira's Woodlawn Cemetery, together with his assistant, provided a simple service. John had made it easier by writing his own obituary, which read in part:

> I came to New York State in 1862, since which time I have been cut off from the church. I have tried to be faithful to the New Testament and the

8 Henry, *History of the Church of the Brethren in Maryland*, 376; Ankrum, *Sidelights on Brethren History*, 119; Ankrum, "Antietam, Maryland, Dunker Bible," 6, 10.

9 Wisbey, Jr., "John T. Lewis, Mark Twain's Friend in Elmira," 1-2; Albert B. Paine, *Mark Twain, A Biography*, 3 vols. (New York, 1912), vol. 2, 515-516.

Grave of John T. Lewis in Woodlawn Cemetery in Elmira, NY. Unmarked for nearly a century, the Brethren Historical Committee of the Church of the Brethren raised funds to mark Lewis' grave. *Nancy Cambpell, Woodlawn Cemetery, Elmira, NY*

order of the Brethren. Though separated from them here, I hope to meet them above where parting is no more. When I am gone, if no brother can be obtained to preach my funeral, I request to be laid away without any ceremony as I recognize none as true Christians who refuse to teach the whole Gospel. Jesus said: 'My sheep hear my voice and another shepherd will they not follow.'[10]

Lewis is buried not far from his Quarry Farm co-worker, antagonist, and sparring partner, "Auntie" Mary Cord, who had died some years earlier in 1888. In another section of Woodlawn Cemetery rests his old friend Mark Twain, who died just four years after Lewis in 1910. Members of the Langdon family, several of whom were saved in 1877 by the heroism of an African American Dunker farmer and Langdon coachman, rest nearby.

10 Henry, *History of the Church of the Brethren in Maryland*, 376-377; Ankrum, *Sidelights on Brethren History*, 122.

Speculation has it that the popular character of "Jim," the runaway slave and Huck Finn's friend in Mark Twain's *Adventures of Huckleberry Finn*, was developed, at least in part, with John T. Lewis in mind.[11]

*   *   *

The members of the little Dunker Church of Antietam battlefield welcomed their altar Bible home with open arms—and just in time for the Christmas season of 1903! The Bible was believed to have been donated to the congregation in 1851 by Daniel Miller, in whose home north of Sharpsburg the little congregation met for some years before building its own meetinghouse. The Good Book began its service in the Mumma Church in 1853 when the building was completed. From 1851 to 1862, and then again from 1903 to about 1914, Brethren Elders Michael Emmert, David Long, John Miller, Daniel Wolf, and John Otto, among others, preached from the Bible's pages. The returned Bible revealed obvious signs of wear and tear. The leather backing had come loose, a portion of the leather cover had been torn away, and the title page with the publication data was missing.[12]

An article about the Antietam battlefield in the September 15, 1907, issue of the *Washington Post* mentions the Dunker Church, the returned Bible, and New Yorker Nathan Dykeman:

> The Dunkard Church is near the Hagerstown pike. It is to-day the same small, single-room brick building that it was in wartime. Several holes made by cannon balls have been repaired, but orifices made by bullets are still to be seen. The rude benches of ante-bellum days are still used at the services held once a month. A precious relic here is a Bible taken from the

11 Thomasson, "Mark Twain and His Dunker Friend," 16-21; Clem, "Civil War Footsteps: Black Farmer Plays Key Role in Return of Dunkard Bible," 14.

12 Clem, "Civil War Footsteps: Black Farmer Plays Key Role in Return of Dunkard Bible," 14; Ankrum, "Antietam, Maryland, Dunker Bible," 5-6, 10; Ankrum, *Sidelights on Brethren History*, 117.

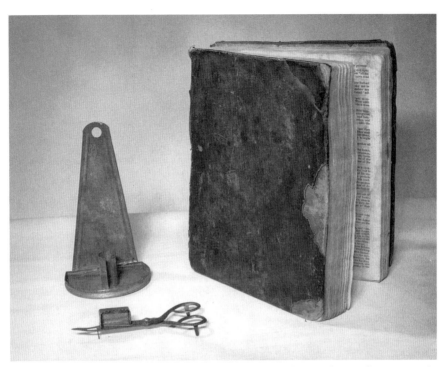

The returned "Antietam Bible" showing its wear and tear along with a candle sconce and scissors for trimming candle or oil lamp wicks. This display was in the Washington County (MD) Historical Society in Hagerstown, MD. *Washington County (MD) Historical Society and ANB*

church after the battle by Nathan Dykman [Dykeman] of Company H, 107th New York Volunteers, and returned in 1903, forty-one years later.[13]

The "Antietam Bible" remained in the Dunker Church until 1914. The Brethren had actually opened a new church in Sharpsburg proper in 1899, and the old battlefield church was being utilized only once a month for a long while until general maintenance and repair of the building and grounds was all but suspended. Many of the church members lived in town and the new church was much more convenient. A deciding factor in closing the Mumma meetinghouse was the constant vandalism to the church building itself. Souvenir hunters regularly pulled bricks from the rear of the building that

13 "State and Nation Have Helped Veterans Adorn Picturesque Antietam Battlefield," *The Washington Post*, September 15, 1907, M8.

Rev. Frank Ramirez, of the Church of the Brethren, in Dunker dress with the "Antietam Bible," normally a part of the annual Brethren commemorative worship service in the Dunker Church. *Alann Schmidt*

had stood witness to the battle of Antietam, further weakening the structure until a hole large enough to enter the church appeared.

Worried that the altar Bible might be taken a second time, church leaders wrapped the book in heavy brown paper and placed it for safekeeping in the vault of the Fahrney-Keedy home, a Brethren facility for the aged in Mapleville, not far from Boonsboro, Maryland. The Bible was taken from the vault in 1937 and displayed during the 75th Anniversary of the battle when President Franklin D. Roosevelt presented the keynote address. It was reported that the brown paper bundle was used as a door stop at one point during renovations at the Fahrney-Keedy home until someone finally unwrapped it only to discover the Dunker Church Bible inside!

The Bible made several temporary stops, including in the Washington County Historical Society in Hagerstown, Maryland, for safekeeping, until early attempts to reconstruct the Dunker Church on the battlefield failed. The Bible became the property of Mr. and Mrs. Newton Long of Baltimore, a grandson of Elder David Long who had preached the worship service in the Mumma meetinghouse on September 14, 1862, just before the battle. Mrs. Long is the great-great-granddaughter of Daniel Miller, who had donated the Bible to the congregation in 1851.

The Dunker Church Bible was later given to the temporary care of Dr. and Mrs. Walter Shealy of Sharpsburg, an officer of the Washington County

Historical Society, who kept it until the National Park Service finally reconstructed the Dunker Church in the 1960s.

Today, the Dunker Church Bible has been repaired and restored and is on display in the museum of the Visitor Center at Antietam National Battlefield. Since 1970, on the Sunday closest to the anniversary of the battle, the "Antietam Bible" has been carried to the reconstructed Dunker Church, where it becomes part of a special commemorative Brethren worship service.[14]

---

14 Ankrum, *Sidelights on Brethren History*, 120-122; Ankrum, "Antietam, Maryland, Dunker Church," 10; Schildt, *Drums Along the Antietam*, 291; Sullivan, "A Battle, A Bundle, & A Black Farmer," at lorilynnsullivan.com/tag/dunkard-Bible; Clem, "Civil War Footsteps: Black Farmer Plays Key Role in Return of Dunkard Bible," 14.

Chapter 8

"God is Again Worshipped in His Sanctuary"

Reverend Austin Cooper detailed the sad and often horrendous activities the Dunkers performed once the Battle of Antietam edged into history:

> Following the battle Brethren and their neighbors helped with the clean-up operations, burying the dead, and binding up the wounds of the fallen brave men. The Church was used as a hospital, embalming room, and amputation station during and after the battle.[1]

He also assessed the overall damage suffered by the Dunker Church, which as it turned out was considerable:

> Thousands of rifle shots had pelted the little church. The end of the roof at the comb facing the Sharpsburg-Hagerstown Pike had been blown away by a shell. At least thirty solids had gone all the way through the church. It was

---

1 Cooper, "A Brief Sketch of the Development of the Reconstruction Project, 1960-1962," 1.

badly damaged and most of the windows had been broken. The roof was pierced hundreds of times with shot.[2]

Many in the congregation felt the little church was damaged beyond repair. Other voiced their fears that the House of the Lord had been thoroughly desecrated by the horrors of war, shattering the peace convictions of the Dunkers. They wanted the church abandoned as a further place of worship.

Samuel Mumma, however, took an opposite view. He argued that the little church should be raised again "as a symbol of peace and goodwill among men of all creeds and differences." A half-dozen families supported him.

A meeting was held at the Mumma Church on October 12, 1863, to discuss the pros and cons of repairing the building. Elder Daniel Reichard, the presiding elder of the Manor congregation, opened the meeting, but it was the "Bishop of all Maryland," Elder Daniel P. Sayler, presiding elder of the Pipe Creek-Beaver Dam congregation, who made the motion that the Mumma Church should be restored, and that worship services should resume as quickly as possible. To help pay for the repairs, Elder Sayler asked that the Brethren in Maryland and throughout the Brotherhood take up offerings in their meetinghouses to help defray the expenses of the Mumma congregation, and "to help the Brethren [there] in need who are suffering from losses because of the war." The vote passed overwhelmingly.

A building committee was promptly organized with specific duties assigned to various Brethren to accomplish the restoration of the Dunker Church. Elder Reichard was made the "general overseer," and Elder Sayler was placed in charge of "fund raising" throughout Maryland and the Brotherhood.

The building committee was appointed by Elder Daniel Reichard and included Henry Neikirk (foreman), John Ecker, Jacob F. Miller, David Otto, Elder David Long, and Daniel Wolf. Noah and John Putnam served as carpenters and plasterers, along with Peter Schamel, a cabinet finisher who put the "last coat on the walls and ceiling of the church. He also did the refinishing to the floor and the woodwork inside the church." Samuel Creamer and David Otto were charged with making new bricks on the Otto

---

2 Cooper, "Upon This Rock—Build," 13.

Brethren Elder Daniel P. Sayler,
the "Bishop of all Maryland," and his wife, Sarah. *BHLA*

A postwar view of the rebuilt and restored Dunker Church. *ANB*

farm, "where the original bricks were made and fired." Finally, Henry Neikirk, John Ecker, and Jacob F. Miller, representing the entire Manor congregation, were appointed trustees of the Mumma Church.[3]

Writing from Double Pipe Creek, Maryland, on February 10, 1864, Elder Daniel P. (D. P.) Sayler informed the denomination of some important news in his letter printed in *The Gospel-Visitor*, the magazine of the Brethren. "The Meetinghouse is also rebuilt, and God is again worshipped in his sanctuary," he proudly reported. Sayler reported that a total of $513.75 had been raised "for the relief of the suffering brethren on 'Antietam Battlefield,' and for the rebuilding of the meetinghouse, which was battered by shells, and much of it carried away by visitors as relics &c." These funds were promptly given to Elder David Long and Valentine Reichard, a deacon, to be "distributed as directed" by the council of the church. "I would further

---

3 Ibid., 14.

inform the brethren that br Mumaw [Mumma] has erected a small house in which he and his family live," added the Elder. "Br Mumaw has not yet recovered his health. His nervous system being much impaired by the shock of battle, &c."[4]

Elder Sayler had made an earlier visit to Washington County to view the damage and losses incurred by the Brethren during Lee's first invasion of the North. He left his home at Double Pipe Creek on Sunday, July 19, 1863, and returned home three days later on the afternoon of Wednesday, July 22. Oddly, he seems not to have ventured as far as Sharpsburg, the battlefield, and the Mumma Church! On July 25, Elder Sayler penned a letter from Double Pipe Creek to *The Gospel-Visitor* detailing his visits with other Brethren in Washington County, including with Elder David Long and his family near Fairplay on Monday, the 20th:

> [I] came to the house of our dear br. D. Long. I found his very interesting family well, and am happy to say his farm was not hurt. His loss is in horses, cattle and hay. His house being between the two lines of pickets, who shot at each other all day, the bullets whizzed by the door and striking the house frequently; but none were hurt.[5]

A letter addressed to the "Brethren Editors" by [Deacon] Valentine Reichard, clerk of the Manor congregation, was printed below Elder Saylor's letter in the March 1864 issue of *The Gospel-Visitor*. On behalf of the Manor congregation, including the Mumma Church, Reichard thanked Elder Sayler for his good work and to all who contributed to the restoration fund and to the suffering Brethren in the area. Valentine Reichard also wrote about the two Confederate invasions of the North, the first ending at Antietam in September 1862, and the second at Gettysburg in July 1863:

> The Manor church has suffered far more than any other church, either in Maryland or Pennsylvania, by the armies. Our entire territory being overrun, and occupied by both armies during the two invasions. The

---

4 Ibid., 13-14; *The Gospel-Visitor* (March 1864), 93-94; after staying with the Sherricks, the Mummas rebuilt their home in the spring of 1863 on the same foundation using the three surviving walls. One assumes that this was the "small house" mentioned by Elder Sayler.

5 *The Gospel-Visitor* (September 1863), 284-287.

territory of the church extends from the South Mountain, a few miles below Boonsboro, west to the Potomac River; with the river north, several miles above Williamsport; then east to Hagerstown; from thence south to Boonsboro and the South Mountain. Brethren who have visited this church will at once understand what portion of the territory was occupied by the two armies at the different invasions —the southern end, when the battle of Antietam was fought, during the first invasion; at the second, the northern end was occupied by both armies. Our losses were consequently heavy, for the Rebel army subsisted entirely off of the country they passed through. But we feel thankful that it is not worse, and if we meet with no further disaster, in a few years our losses will not be seriously felt.[6]

Thus it becomes clear that the repairs to the Dunker Church were completed before Elder Sayler's letter of February 10, 1864. The actual date of the church rededication has not been ascertained with certainty. According to Rev. Cooper, Fred Peterman related that his father, James Peterman, told him it was held in the afternoon on the first Sunday in January 1864. Elder Daniel Reichard reportedly preached the rededication sermon entitled "Upon This Rock—Build." The following is a transcription from a small volume in which James Peterman had written. His son Fred allowed Rev. Cooper to copy it:

A very large crowd was in attendance and the singing the best ever heard by this servant. Not much was said about the war and the terrible suffering all around us but the elder spoke quietly and directly about how much more we all have to live the peace that Christ preached and taught by his living in that day. We must pray for our brothers and our sons who are away from home and for all those who are caught in this terrible war. The elder spoke about the new church as it stands on this hill how it must remain a light on the hill for all the world to see. He also spoke how symbolic it is that this church stands right by the side of this important road. Every member and every Christian must let his light shine for truth and peace.[7]

---

6   Valentine Reichard to the "Brethren Editors," The Gospel-Visitor (March 1864), 93-94.

7   Cooper, "Upon This Rock—Build," 14.

President Abraham Lincoln, facing General George B. McClellan, with other Union officers photographed in front of the Grove house at Sharpsburg on Friday, October 3, 1862—the same day Lincoln reportedly stopped at the Dunker Church while touring the battlefield. *LOC*

President Abraham Lincoln visited the Antietam battlefield October 1-4, 1862. During Lincoln's tour of the battlefield—probably on Friday, October 3—his entourage reportedly stopped at the Dunker Church, where the president is said to have stood on the blue limestone steps to better address a group of civilians and soldiers gathered there. Once he finished, the president visited inside with the wounded of both sides.

One Union veteran, a 16-year-old private named Calvin H. Blanchard, who served with Company D of the 111th Pennsylvania Infantry, later claimed he was one of the wounded inside the church when Lincoln visited, and that he got to meet both "President and Mrs. Lincoln." Mary Todd Lincoln, however, did not accompany her husband on his trip to Antietam, having instead remained in the White House in Washington. Blanchard may have seen a woman there with the president, but if so, who did he see? Almost certainly we will never know, but it may have been Clara Barton, "the Angel of the Battlefield" and founder of the American Red Cross. In all likelihood, however, the woman was probably a local helping care for the wounded, possibly even a Dunker woman.[8]

Union General Jacob D. Cox was with the Lincoln party when it toured the Antietam battlefield. The entourage, explained Cox, started from McClellan's headquarters (the actual site of which appears to be in some question) and followed the same basic route traversed by Major General Edwin Sumner's Second Corps across Antietam Creek, through the East Woods, down the Smoketown Road below D. R. Miller's Cornfield, and to the Dunker Church. From their, the party moved down to the "Bloody Lane" before finally returning to McClellan's headquarters. President Lincoln stayed in the Sharpsburg area for several days reviewing his troops, visiting

---

8 Ankrum, *Sidelights on Brethren History*, 100, 105-106; Schildt, *Drums Along the Antietam*, 253-254; Schildt, *Four Days in October*, 25, 27, 44; Charles William Harman, "Restoration of Old Dunkard Church Planned at Antietam," *Morning* [Hagerstown] *Herald*, March 3, 1937. Private Blanchard had been wounded at Cedar Mountain in Virginia on August 9, 1862. Thanks to Nick Picerno of Bridgewater, VA, for checking his Union database for Blanchard's service record. See also, Edward S. Delaplaine, *Lincoln's Companions on the Trip to Antietam* (Harrogate, TN, 1954) and E. Russell Hicks, "The Church on the Battlefield," part two, *Gospel Messenger* (February 9, 1952), 14. It is believed that Clara Barton visited the Dunker Church "the day after the battle, and had the wounded removed to her tents some distance away. The hospital units she put into operation at Antietam became later the Red Cross organization of America."

the wounded of both sides in the many field hospitals, and talking with everyone he could.[9]

As may be expected, a number of Christian denominations claim that President Lincoln was baptized and became a member of their order. The Brethren are no exception. Unfortunately, the evidence—thin as it is, and second and even third-hand, at best—does not need to be retold here.[10]

---

9 Schildt, *Drums Along the Antietam*, 292; see also Jacob D. Cox, *Military Reminiscences of the Civil War* (New York, 1900); Sears, *Landscape Turned Red: The Battle of Antietam*, 323-325; Schildt, *Four Days In October*, 25, 27, 44.

10 Ankrum, *Sidelights on Brethren History*, 105, 140-142; Schildt, *Drums Along the Antietam*, 294; Freeman Ankrum, *Maryland and Pennsylvania Historical Sketches* (West Newton, PA, 1947), 37-38. Elder Daniel P. Sayler was apparently a friend to Lincoln and even visited him in the White House. One report claims that President Lincoln promised that he would join the order of the Brethren once the Civil War was over, but again the evidence is weak. However, it does appear that Abraham Lincoln had a certain affinity for the Brethren and similar "peace" groups.

Chapter 9

Battlefield Adornment, Antietam Slaves, and the Demise of the Dunker Church

An unsigned article in the *Washington Post* printed on September 15, 1907, announced that the "state and nation have helped veterans adorn picturesque Antietam Battlefield." It continued:

> National and state cooperation with the veterans who participated in the battle, the most sanguinary single-day encounter of the Civil War, has within the past several years resulted in making the battlefield near Sharpsburg, Md., one of the most elaborately adorned of any in the country. Visitors to the field on Wednesday, the forty-fourth anniversary of the conflict, will find there fifty fine monuments, not including markers, may read the story of the struggle upon 243 cast-iron tablets, and while traveling along the excellent pikes for which the vicinity is famous or the avenues constructed by the national government, keep in the right direction by the aid of 130 cast-iron guide signs.

The article mentioned that Pennsylvania had the most monuments and markers for their soldiers, and that six inverted twelve-pound cannon imbedded in rock and placed by the government marked the sites where six general officers were killed or mortally wounded, three Union (Isaac Rodman, Israel Richardson, and Joseph Mansfield), and three Confederate (Lawrence O'Brien Branch, George Anderson, and William Stark). The major sites and monuments on the Antietam and South Mountain battlefields are mentioned in the article, including the Dunker Church, which at that time was still the original church building. The returned altar Bible in the church was also mentioned.

The piece concluded with a discussion about the National Cemetery at Antietam. The cemetery was founded privately, but since 1877 had been in the possession and care of the United States. The total number of Union bodies buried there was given as 4,734, of which 1,865 were among "the unknown dead." The result, lauded the paper, was magnificent: "The splendid co-operation . . . of nation, states and individuals has effected a wonderful transformation in the vicinity of the old fashioned town of Sharpsburg around which the battlefield lies.[1]

Many of the battlefield monuments were erected where the units served on the battlefield. These markers near the Dunker Church include, for example, monuments for the 125th Pennsylvania and 15th Massachusetts. However, many were not placed where its unit specifically fought, but in the general vicinity on the field where park visitors would actually see them. As a result, many of the battlefield's monuments were put close to the Dunker Church, especially some of the larger state monuments. A road ran past the iconic structure, which was one of the most notable and identifiable on the entire battlefield. Everyone who drove past the church would see them.

Land ownership was another important factor affecting tourism. Other than the National Cemetery, during the early years there was no federally owned land at Antietam. Individual groups bought land on their own. New York, for example, bought a plot and erected a rather large monument, as did Maryland (the only monument on the entire battlefield dedicated to both sides). The Philadelphia Brigade bought a large plot and made it a park area. When the War Department established the national battlefield in 1890, it even made a new road (Confederate Avenue) through the West Woods to make it easier for tourists to get around the sprawling field.[2]

---

1   "State and Nation Have Helped Veterans Adorn Picturesque Antietam Battlefield," *The Washington Post*, September 15, 1907. The Confederate dead were eventually buried in "local," non-federal government cemeteries in Hagerstown and Frederick, Maryland, and in Shepherdstown, Virginia, now West Virginia. "Antietam," Antietam National Battlefield, MD, reprint 2009.

2   Susan W. Trail, *Remembering Antietam*: *Commemoration and Preservation of a Civil War Battlefield*, Ph.D. dissertation (College Park, MD, 2005).

Members of the 125th Pennsylvania in reunion at the Dunker Church in 1888. This unit had its baptism of fire in the West Woods. *ANB*

An article in the *Cincinnati Daily Gazette* dated September 21, 1867, explained how the Dunker Church was rededicated in 1867 on the fifth anniversary of the battle. By this time The Brethren had repaired and rededicated the church in 1864, so this 1867 "rededication" is somewhat puzzling. Calling the little church "beautiful" for a wayside place, the correspondent added, "it has been entirely repaired and painted, though you can see new pieces set in where the solid shot burst in the gable and eaves."[3]

A small 15" x 18" cast-iron tablet was mounted by the War Department in the 1890s just to the right of the "front" or east door of the Dunker Church. After the church was blown down in a windstorm in 1921, the wording on the tablet was placed on an aluminum plaque mounted on an iron pipe and erected next to the foundation of the building. It read as follows:

THE DUNKARD CHURCH

Erected A. D. 1853 By The German Baptist Brethren. During The Battle The Wounded of Both Armies Sought And Found Sanctuary Within Its Walls. The Church Was Seriously Injured By The Fire Of The Union Batteries On September 17, 1862. The Building Was Repaired And Divine Worship Was Resumed During The Summer of 1864.[4]

Another memorial to the Dunker Church was erected in 1927. An elderly O. T. "Pop" Reilly, the battlefield's first tour guide and a man who truly loved the Dunker Church, had a small monument erected across the road (Dunker Church Road) from where the Visitor Center is today. The inscription reads:

To the memory of the old Dunkard Church, the oak tree that stood in front, and the Union Civil War Veterans of Sharpsburg, Md.[5]

---

3 *Cincinnati Daily Gazette*, September 21, 1867; see Reardon and Vossler, *A Field Guide to Antietam*, 130, 326.

4 Schildt, *Drums Along the Antietam*, 288; Louis E. Tuckerman, *Report of the Old Dunkard Church and Site at Antietam National Battlefield Site, Sharpsburg, Maryland, August 1951*, 17.

5 Alexander, "Forgotten Valor: Off the Beaten Path at Antietam," 16. In the 1960s, the Washington County Historical Society came up with a plan to use wood from felled trees

Oliver T. (O. T.) Reilly who served as "the official guide for Antietam and South Mountain battlefields, having 50 years' experience," told the story of some returning veterans of the battle in 1895, apparently all Confederate artillerymen, led by a "Major Parker." When the touring group reached the Dunker Church, the aging Rebels walked to their respective artillery positions near the church before coming together again to kneel and pray—the only time O. T. Reilly ever saw any returning veterans do that on the battlefield.[6]

Dr. Emmert Bittinger, a retired professor of sociology at Bridgewater College in Virginia—a Brethren-related college—was also a prominent Brethren and Mennonite historian who served as pastor of the Sharpsburg Church of the Brethren for seven years (1951-1958). Emmert, who as of this writing is 91, served on the committee for the rebuilding and rededication of the Dunker Church. He offered several fascinating stories from his time in Sharpsburg:

> . . . in the 1950s the Burnside bridge was still being used for vehicle travel. I crossed it twice every Sunday plus extra times when I did pastoral visits during the week. I must have made close to seven hundred crossings.

> An interesting historical artifact is located on the street corner a dozen or two yards up from the Sharpsburg Church. Little attention is paid to it by most people because they do not know what it is. It is a stone step-stone used in slave-holding times for slaves to step up and stand on the stand so prospective buyers could better see the slave they were bidding on. Often they would be nearly nude, so the bidders could see how badly their backs were scarred from the beating they had received from their masters—

---

from around the Dunker Church to make "keys to the city" for Hagerstown. Wood from around the original Jonathan Hager home in Hagerstown would also be used. See "New 'Keys' Are Designed for City: Wood from Historical Dunker Church, Hager Home to be Used," *Morning* [Hagerstown] *Herald*, date unknown, Antietam National Battlefield Library Collection.

6 Reilly, "Stories of Antietam"; Schildt, *Drums Along the Antietam*, 292; William A. Frassanito, *Antietam: The Photographic Legacy of America's Bloodiest Day* (New York, 1978), 160-164. Major Parker was probably Captain William W. Parker of Parker's (Richmond) Virginia Battery. As noted earlier, the Confederate dead captured in Alexander Gardner's iconic images near the abandoned limber chest with the dead horse in front of the Dunker Church were reported to be mostly men from Parker's Virginia Battery.

The Dunker Church, photographed about the turn of the twentieth century. Note the swing hanging in the tree on the left. This image originally belonged to O. T. Reilly, the battlefield's first tour guide. *Nicholas P. Picerno*

enabling the bidders to estimate the behavior of the slave. This artifact is located at a vulnerable location, as a turning truck or car could damage it.

Some of the older members could still recall stories of the battle. For example, Mr. [Philip] Lum, 90 years of age, who lived across the street from the Sharpsburg Church told how after the terrible battle, citizens searched among the bodies for money or anything of value in the pockets of the dead soldiers.

You would know, of course, that the Dunker Church was used as a hospital. After cutting off a foot, leg or arm, the assistants would throw them out the church windows to eventually be hauled away. The pile of limbs would become so large that they would fall back into the building. Mr. Lum also told that one of his uncles had retrieved a small 'soldiers Bible' from a soldier's coat, which he gave to me. After many years, I presented it to the Antietam Battlefield Museum.[7]

Whether there is a "slave block" in Sharpsburg is a matter of some controversy. A plaque on the face of the step-stone in question denotes it as the "Old Slave Block," based upon local tradition. Current scholarship contends the step-stone (there is reportedly another on the square) was merely used for stepping into a carriage or onto a horse, and was not a slave block at all.

At any rate, the slave block/step-stone in Sharpsburg mentioned by Dr. Bittinger illustrates the complexity of the divisive issue of slavery amongst the populace of Maryland, a border state between North and South. As pointed out earlier, even the Brethren had their problems with the issue as a few themselves owned slaves. Some Dunkers would buy slaves and set them free. Elder David Long of the Manor Church, who preached the sermon in the Mumma Church on the Sunday before the battle, is reported to have done exactly that.[8]

---

7 Email from Dr. Emmert Bittinger to Terry Barkley, August 23, 2016; co-author interview with Emmert and Esther Bittinger at Bridgewater Retirement Community, Bridgewater, VA, August 30, 2016.

8 Ankrum, *Sidelights on Brethren History*, 115.

Two Dunkers in the Sharpsburg area who owned slaves were Samuel Mumma and John Otto. The Mummas had two slaves they manumitted (freed) in 1856: Lucy Young and Lloyd Wilson. In 1850, Lucy was recorded as being 28, and Lloyd only two. Lloyd was 13 at the time of the battle and 15 in 1864 when the new Maryland constitution finally freed slaves in that state. Lincoln's Emancipation Proclamation only applied to those slaves living in the rebellion states. Slave-holding states like Maryland, Kentucky, Missouri, and Delaware were border states that never seceded, and thus exempted. It appears the pious Samuel and Elizabeth Mumma actually had manumission in mind from the very beginning.

John Otto (his wife Dorcus had died in 1844) owned two slaves, reportedly a mother and her son, Aunt Nancy and Hilary Watson. Though exempt from the Emancipation Proclamation, John Otto and his second wife Katherine (Gardnouer) honored the spirit of Lincoln's declaration by freeing their slaves in early 1863. Soon after, when Hilary was drafted into the Union army, John Otto took him to Frederick, Maryland, and paid $300 for an exemption. After the war Hilary served as a trustee at Tolson's Chapel

(Methodist), an African-American church in Sharpsburg founded in 1866. In 1868, he helped found a Freedmen's Bureau school known as the "American Union" school, which opened in the church. Hilary died in 1917 at the age of 85 and was buried in the little cemetery behind Tolson's Chapel.[9]

At the Roulette farm near the Sunken Road or "Bloody Lane," William and Margaret Ann (Miller)

The graves of Hilary and Christiana Watson in the little cemetery behind Tolson's Chapel in Sharpsburg, Maryland.
Dr. Jeff Bach

9   Tolson's Chapel served the African-American community in Sharpsburg for 132 years (1866 to 1998). The Freedmen's Bureau school opened in the church in 1868 with eighteen students; twelve had been slaves.

Tolson's Chapel (1866-1998), an African-American church and Freedmen's Bureau school in Sharpsburg, Maryland. *Tolson's Chapel, Sharpsburg, MD*

Roulette and their family were served by two free blacks (the Roulettes supposedly never owned slaves). Nancy Campbell was 40 in 1860, and Robert Simon a 15-year-old farm hand. Nancy accompanied the Roulette family members when they left for the Manor Church north of Sharpsburg to escape the battle, though William Roulette returned to his home and was caught between the battle lines before finally escaping. Nancy, who was loved and cared for as a member of the Roulette family, stayed with the Roulettes for the rest of her life until she died in September 1892. She was a member of the Manor Church and is buried in the Manor cemetery. Nancy was also active at Tolson's Chapel, the African-American church in Sharpsburg. She donated a pulpit Bible to it that is displayed in the museum of the Visitor Center at the battlefield. Nancy, who never married, donated $20 each to the Manor Church and Tolson's Chapel, before leaving her tidy

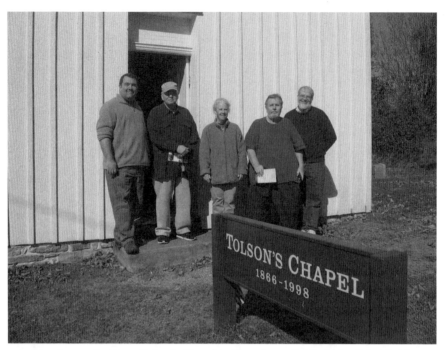

An October 2016 visit to Tolson's Chapel in Sharpsburg. (L-R): Alann Schmidt, Terry Barkley, Edie Wallace (Tolson's Chapel), Ted Alexander, and Dr. Jeff Bach. *Dr. Jeff Bach*

estate of some $800 to the children of the Roulette and Miller families. Her Manumission Paper or certificate is also on display at the battlefield Visitor Center, along with other memorabilia associated with the Roulette family.

Jeremiah (Jerry) Summers was a slave on the Piper farm at the time of the battle and accompanied the family when the Pipers left their home seeking safety from the fighting. The Pipers were of the German Reformed faith. Manumitted in 1864 when all slaves in Maryland were freed, Jerry elected to stay with the Pipers and work for them. He died in 1925 at age 76, and was buried in the cemetery behind Tolson's Chapel.

Finally, it is known that David R. Miller, whose farm included the famous Cornfield, owned one female slave in 1860.[10]

10 One report claims the Roulettes freed their one slave in 1859. Ernst, *Too Afraid To Cry*, 225; Walker and Kirkman, "Samuel Mumma Farm," 74, 102-103, 107; "Contradictions and Divided Loyalties, Slavery on the Antietam Battleground: A Companion Guide to the Auto Tour for School Groups," www.nps.gov/anti/learn/education/upload/Contradictions-and-

* * *

In April of 1913, Senator John W. Smith of Maryland alerted the War Department that the Dunker Church might be sold. War Department officials decided that, if at all possible, the church should be acquired as a "historic shrine," although they also suggested the structure could be used as an "office for the Superintendent or storehouse for tools." On September 17 of that same year, $1,500 was included in the budget for the upcoming fiscal year to purchase the church and surrounding lot. Congress appropriated the requested funds, but the property owners decided not to sell and the money went back into the U.S. Treasury.[11]

As the years passed, only sporadic services were conducted in the church. Adequate repair and maintenance were routinely left undone on the historic building. The routine practice of souvenir hunters taking bricks from the church's walls continued to weaken the small building. Unfortunately, time was running out for the historic structure. A severe windstorm swept through the Antietam Valley on May 23, 1921, and the old church collapsed into a heap of rubble. Fortunately, it was empty at the time and no one was killed or injured. The storm caused other damage across the area, including the destruction of several fields of ripening wheat and shattered windows in a number of farmhouses. None of this damage, however, was as significant as the destruction of the Dunker Church. While the storm was dangerous on its own, the damage done by vandals, piled onto the lingering effects of damage inflicted during the battle, played an important role in the church's demise.[12]

The pile of unsightly rubble became an immediate attraction in and of itself. Visitors from near and far flocked to the site to view the damage, and many scooped up bricks and other items as souvenirs, further diluting the integrity of the former building's historic components. The Quartermaster General of the War Department recommended that $1,200 be included in the

Divided-Loyalties.pdf; Tolson's Chapel, Sharpsburg, MD, http://www.tolsonschapel.org/; Email from Dr. Jeff Bach to Terry Barkley, September 19, 2016.

11 Charles W. Snell and Sharon Brown, *Antietam National Battlefield and National Cemetery, Sharpsburg, Maryland: An Administrative History* (Washington, D.C., 1986), 127.

12 Robert L. Lagemann, *Historic Structures Report for the Dunkard Church, Antietam National Battlefield, May 25, 1960*, 38.

The ruins of the Dunker Church after it was blown down in a severe windstorm on May 23, 1921. *ANB*

Another view of the ruins of the Dunker Church, with unnamed visitors on the right. *ANB*

Elmer Boyer, who bought the Dunker Church property and the ruins on it, with one of church's salvaged pews. *ANB*

1924 budget to purchase the church property, but the money was not available and the budget moved forward without it. That same year, a congressman from the local district introduced a bill to authorize the rebuilding of the church. Nothing came of it and the bill was never enacted.

Since the local Church of the Brethren had already built a new facility in town in 1899, and had not been using the old church for a long time, it had neither the need for it, nor the interest in reconstructing it. The Brethren did agree, however, that the property should revert back to the Mumma family, as stipulated in the original indenture (deed) so many year ago. Eventually, Fifty-six Mumma heirs reestablished title to the property in February 1924, and it was put up for auction on May 13, 1925.[13]

13 Axel Axelson, "Visiting Old Battle Fields," *Confederate Veteran* (November 1926), 418. One report concluded that evidence had been found that someone had camped on the church grounds and used one of the window frames as firewood; Snell and Brown, *Antietam National Battlefield and National Cemetery, Sharpsburg, Maryland: An Administrative History*, 127; Benjamin H. Davis, *Completion Report—Reconstruction of Dunkard Church Building (Furnishings), Antietam National Battlefield Site, Sharpsburg, Maryland, November 30, 1962*, 1.

Sharpsburg grocer Elmer Boyer purchased the property and the ruins on it for $800. He salvaged the remaining material and stored it in his garage and outbuildings before selling the property to Charles Turner in 1926 for $400. Turner built a one-story frame building on the original church foundation in 1928. This structure was used as a lunch stand and filling station for years. In 1930, the idea of acquiring the Dunker Church lot and reconstructing the building was briefly revived, but nothing came from the proposal.[14]

14 Lagemann, *Historic Structures Report for the Dunkard Church, Antietam National Battlefield, May 25, 1960*, 11, 13, 39, 58.

Chapter 10

Starts and Stops:
Initial Efforts to Rebuild the Dunker Church

When the National Park Service took over the administration of the battlefield from the War Department in 1933, several studies and reports were compiled on the status and potential of the park in general, and the Dunker Church in particular.

Nearly every report on the subject filed with Superintendent J. K. Beckenbaugh in 1934 mentioned the church and lamented its loss from the field's historical presentation. In a report entitled "Justification for Improvements at Antietam," Carlton Godlove noted, "At present the Dunker Church site is occupied by a soft-drink and lunch stand. Unsightly advertisements cover the frame building, which stands on the old foundation, bearing such signs as 'Drink Coca-Cola,' 'Ice Cold Beer,' etc. I would suggest immediate acquisition of this site and the ground immediately surrounding it, together with the re-building of the church."[1]

Park Service member John O'Connell, Jr. took these sentiments further in his detailed report. The structure located on the church foundation, he observed, is not be utilized as intended at the present time, but it was being used:

---

1 Snell and Brown, *Antietam National Battlefield and National Cemetery, Sharpsburg, Maryland: An Administrative History*, 129.

The lunch stand and later gas station that once stood on the foundation of the Dunker Church. *ANB*

as a refreshment stand in the summer months. The general appearance is abject and unsightly. Instead of the expected quiet, peaceful country church, the visitor is greeted by:

Stop at Turner's Lunch Room
Beechnut Chewing Tobacco
Ham, Egg, and Cheese Sandwiches
Ice Cold Coca-Cola
See Endless Caverns
Ice Cold Beer

There were "similar desecrations," complained O'Connell of the National Park Service. He continued:

The property is owned by a person named Turner, whose residence adjoins the church property. The property was purchased by the present owner for about $400. Reliable information indicates he now values the property at $1700, a ridiculous figure. The restoration of the church is questionably desirable. For years it stood as an unpretentious, silent memorial to those that died on or about its grounds. Complete restoration to its original form is recommended. By virtue of its architecture, this could be accomplished for a very reasonable figure. An effort is being made to obtain specifications, descriptions, photographs, etc. of the old church and to supplement such data with available information that will be of assistance in the re-landscaping of the grounds to conform with the appearance before the battle.[2]

Jordan Bean, also of the National Park Service, summarized the situation in his detailed report: "If this little place could be rebuilt, it would become one of the most interesting places on the battlefield." Despite all of the positive sentiment, funding was simply not made available to implement any of the recommendations—a recurring theme throughout the nearly forty years that the Dunker Church would be absent from the Antietam Battlefield.[3]

The importance of the church to the Battle of Antietam did not diminish as the years passed. The Antietam Celebration Commission prepared a lavish invitation for President Franklin Roosevelt in hope he would attend the 75th Anniversary festivities, including brief background material on the battle and its importance. It included only a few photographs, but among them was one of the old Dunker Church. Despite the brevity of information, the Commission included the following caption under the church picture: "The many suggestions for its restoration as a part of the commemorative movement are most appropriate." The Commission, which was made up of senators, generals, and historians, had one brief chance to get the president's

---

2   Carlton Godlove, "Justification for the Improvements for Antietam," February 8, 1934, 1, Antietam National Battlefield Library.

3   Ibid., 7.

attention, and when they did, they highlighted the important need for the church to be rebuilt.[4]

As the anniversary neared, the Washington County Historical Society decided to take matters into its own hands. At a meeting in March 1937, members decided to undertake a plan to rebuild the church, declaring, "The hallowed surroundings of the battlefield are peculiarly incomplete without the little old church." The society also had a plan for overcoming the problem of funding. The group considered Mr. Turner's asking price for the property exorbitant, and got around it by obtaining an option on more affordable land near where the original church had once stood. The alternate plot was supposedly located so as to not detract from the church's positional association with other landmarks involved in that part of the battle.[5]

The Hagerstown *Morning Herald* reported on April 3, 1937, that a local architect had donated his services to the project and that an application had been filed authorizing the necessary labor to be furnished under a Works Progress Administration (WPA) project. While the specifics on fund-raising were still somewhat unclear, the Historical Society was "confident that the historic old landmark will, before September, resume its place among the many points of interest on the battlefield." Unfortunately, this was not to be. The funding needed was not received, and the plan was never implemented. The salvaged materials from the Dunker Church were displayed at the fairgrounds in Hagerstown, but nothing more was done. After the proposed project for the 75th anniversary fell through, more than a decade passed before the subject of rebuilding the church even arose again.[6]

In 1950, the Maryland state highway administration planned several improvements to the Hagerstown Pike, one of which involved widening the road. This effort would allow the "new" road—the main road in the area—to handle much more traffic. The new route, however, would come within

---

4 Antietam Celebration Commission invitation sent to President Franklin D. Roosevelt to attend and speak at the 75th anniversary of the battle, Antietam National Battlefield Library.

5 Charles William Harman, "Restoration of Old Dunkard Church Planned at Antietam," *Morning* [Hagerstown] *Herald*, March 3, 1937.

6 Ibid., April 3, 1937. While it was admirable that the Washington County Historical Society realized the importance of the Dunker Church and wished to rebuild it, one has to wonder what impact a replacement church would have had erected on land other than the original location.

twenty feet of the church's foundation. Superintendent Doust quickly launched several efforts to bring the matter to the attention of the public.[7]

In October of that year, Doust attended a meeting of the Washington County Historical Society to discuss the issues raised by the new road project. He suggested the group put pressure on the state to acquire the property along with the idea of presenting it to the battlefield for preservation. Doust also attempted to get the local American Legion interested in the project. By early 1951, National Park Service Chief Historian Ronald Lee took an active interest in the developing situation. Lee wrote to the Director of the National Council of Historic Sites and Buildings about the impending threat to the church site, noting, "the National Park Service has long been conscious of the importance of the Dunker Church."[8]

The Washington County Historical Society increased its efforts to purchase the site and entered into negotiations with the Turners. On May 1, 1951, the Hagerstown *Evening Star* reported that the group had purchased the Dunker Church land tract (.30 acre) for $4,000. This was a hefty sum to pay for the land (similar properties had been assessed for tax purposes at just $200), but the Dunker Church site had, at last, been acquired. Society President Dr. Walter Shealy wrote to National Park Service Director Arthur E. Demaray and officially offered to transfer the church site to the agency on Memorial Day. Demaray was pleased by the offer, noting, "the National Park Service was authorized under Act of Congress, approved May 14, 1951, (54 Statute 212) to accept this property." During Memorial Day services at the Antietam National Cemetery, Dr. Shealy formally presented the deed to the National Park Service. While no specific commitment was made by the Battlefield Administration that the church itself would be rebuilt, it was made very clear that everyone involved wished to do so.[9]

Meanwhile, park staff worked to find a way to rebuild the church. Staff Historian Louis Tuckerman compiled a lengthy report on the importance of

---

7 Snell and Brown, *Antietam National Battlefield and National Cemetery, Sharpsburg, Maryland: An Administrative History*, 210.

8 Ibid., 252; Ronald F. Lee to Frederick L Rath, Jr., National Council for Historic Sites and Buildings, February 16, 1951, Antietam National Battlefield Library.

9 Snell and Brown, *Antietam National Battlefield and National Cemetery, Sharpsburg, Maryland: An Administrative History*, 253; *Evening* [Hagerstown] *Star*, May 1, 1951. The legally required title search conducted by the U.S. Government took about two years to complete, so the Dunker Church site was not legally accepted until April 15, 1953.

the church. He came to many of the same conclusions reached by historians from the 1930s, including the fact that, "even today, certain modern park roads and practically all former and current battle accounts are oriented to a strategically placed building which no longer exists." His report detailed the background of the Dunker Church, as well as many practical considerations for the park in relation to rebuilding the structure. It also included a listing of the many benefits a rebuilt church would bring the park in terms of tourism. Tuckerman called these "Publicity Potential Points."

Tuckerman noted that many original parts of the building were still in existence; Elmer Boyer still owned them nearly four decades after he salvaged what he could from the church wreckage. "A restored building," Tuckerman noted, "could be presented to the public as 'almost the original.'" Tuckerman and Superintendent Doust visited with Boyer to see the various pieces stored at his Sharpsburg home in his garage loft, a small barn, and anywhere he could find space for them. The remains, Tuckerman explained, had been stored in a "haphazard manner," but they had been well protected from the weather and were in reasonably good shape. Boyer had also kept insurance coverage on the items during all those years.[10]

Despite the limited funds, Tuckerman continued negotiating to acquire the materials. The effort was frustrating experience. In a memo to Doust dated August 1, 1951, Tuckerman related that Boyer's asking price for the collection was $7,500— an amount Tuckerman considered vulgarly excessive. Boyer, he opined, had been influenced by the high price the Washington County Historical Society had paid for the Dunker Church site. For a short time, Tuckerman and Doust considered moving ahead with the project without Boyer's original materials by developing a museum inside the rebuilt church instead of recreating the interior, or even just finishing the outside appearance of the building and not having anything on the inside.[11]

By August 8 that same year, Superintendent Doust was able to write to Chief Historian Ronald Lee that the project was progressing, Tuckerman's

---

10 Ibid., 260; Tuckerman, *Report of the Old Dunkard Church and Site at Antietam National Battlefield Site, Sharpsburg, Maryland, August 1951*, 1, 28-29. See also, Louis Tuckerman, "Dunkard Church Property," August 1, 1951, 1.

11 Tuckerman, *Report of the Old Dunkard Church and Site at Antietam National Battlefield Site, Sharpsburg, Maryland, August 1951*, 1, 20. Louis Tuckerman memorandum to Superintendent, Antietam National Battlefield Site, August 1, 1951. Antietam National Battlefield Library.

report was finished, and the structure that was on the church foundation had been removed. In addition, negotiations to buy the surrounding land, as well as the Boyer materials, were moving along. The following March, 1952, a meeting was held in Sharpsburg regarding the reconstruction and preservation of the Dunker Church. Many regional National Park Service officials were in attendance, including the chief historian, regional architect, and the superintendent of Gettysburg National Military Park, as well as Tuckerman and Doust. The group concluded that, while the process of rebuilding the church was being considered and planned, the site should be stabilized and protected. They also contacted the Washington County Historical Society to provide assistance in searching for any photos of the original church to help in planning a new structure. When it was discovered that no photos were available that showed the rear of the building, society members placed several newspaper articles encouraging citizens to share any available photos or info with them.[12]

Once again, however, the effort to the rebuild the Dunker Church hit a roadblock. Even though the Battlefield staff and historical society were pushing ahead, the project was promptly squashed by Regional Director Ronald Cox. "Tuckerman's report was valuable," explained Cox in a letter to Gettysburg Superintendent James W. Coleman,

> but additional architectural study must be made before plans and a complete estimate are prepared. We estimate a complete reconstruction would cost in excess of $50,000. Although we have indicated interest in the possible reconstruction of this historic building, the question immediately arises as to how valuable such a project would be, and whether, in the face of such a high cost, we could give it any priority in our construction program. In discussing it here, we are of the opinion that this project would have to fall below many others in priority in the region. I am aware of the interest which community organizations have in this project and we would not want to discourage them in their efforts. However, unless they are willing and able to undertake the project, I believe that we should tell them frankly of our situation. In other words, it is not fair to let them go on believing and hoping that we will do something about the project when

12 Snell and Brown, *Antietam National Battlefield and National Cemetery, Sharpsburg, Maryland: An Administrative History*, 261.

The foundation of the Dunker Church with a temporary sign erected until the permanent aluminum signage could be installed. *ANB*

really the prospects of getting money to do the job are almost hopeless. Certainly that is the picture as I see it.[13]

Cox's letter ruined any hope of rebuilding the church in the near future, primarily because of his extremely high estimate ($50,000) of the project's cost. (The Korean War was in also progress, which made it even more difficult to obtain funds for any project.) Cox's high estimate, coupled with his assertion that the Dunker Church was not significant enough to warrant such a high price, ended the matter. The park, however, did stabilize the foundation. Instead of rebuilding the church, it erected a marker.

It appeared as though the old Dunker Church was really gone, never to return.[14]

13 Ibid., 262. Ten years later in 1962, when the church was reconstructed, the cost was less than $20,000.

14 Ibid., 263-265.

Chapter 11

A New Day for the Dunker Church

And so the years passed, leaving the battlefield without its most noted landmark. As the automobile industry grew and many Americans set out to see the country, tourism across the nation flourished. Those who drove to Antietam to learn about America's bloodiest single-day battle, however, left without seeing an essential part of the story. They could walk down Bloody Lane, and even drive over the Burnside Bridge (at least until 1964), but where the Dunker Church had once stood, only a bare foundation remained.

Sentiment to rebuild the church, however, continued to smolder. Letters to the editor published in local newspapers lamented the church's absence. One, penned by Mrs. May Shank dated April 18, 1958, listed several reasons she did not approve of the Federal government buying more land at Antietam. One of them was because it had not seen fit to rebuild the Dunker Church.

In a letter to the Antietam National Battlefield, Rev. Austin Cooper, the Church of the Brethren minister and historian who had been very active in the rebuilding campaign opened with a question: "What must people in other states think of the citizens of Hagerstown and Washington County when they realize that, for nearly a decade, we have neglected to replace an inexpensive building which every historian mentions in writing of the conflict near Sharpsburg?" He continued: "Citizens of Washington County now know that they can easily replace the shot-riddled structure that is missed by thousands of tourists, and we are quite sure they will not care to

Reenactment of the September 14, 1862, worship service held in the Mumma Church before the battle. Sponsored by the Church of the Brethren, this was phase one of the "Goodwill on the Battlefield" pageant held on September 7, 1958. *ANB*

endure reproach of continued neglect of so famous a shrine within the county's borders."[1]

The Church of the Brethren decided to take action by staging a pageant on the foundation of the church on September 7, 1958. The pageant was entitled "Goodwill on the Battlefield," and was the official kickoff of a campaign by the organization to restore the Dunker Church as a peace shrine. Several hundred spectators watched the three-part event.

Part one took place on the foundation of the church and was a reenactment of the September 14, 1862, service on the day of the Battle of South Mountain. Parts two and three were conducted on the hill between the foundation and the New York monument and included, respectively, reenactments of Clara Barton's medical operations and President Lincoln's post-battle visit. At the conclusion of the pageant, two white doves representing peace were released. The Middle Maryland District of the Church of the Brethren arranged the event, and many other local churches

1 *Morning* [Hagerstown] *Herald*, April 18, 1958; undated letter from Rev. Austin Cooper to Antietam National Battlefield, Antietam National Battlefield Library.

participated. A 100-voice choir provided music, and E. Russell Hicks and Rev. Freeman Ankrum prepared the historical presentations. The pageant was well-attended and brought a considerable amount of publicity to the rebuilding effort.[2]

The bright light of media attention continued to shine on the plight of the Dunker Church when, in April 1959, a House of Representatives task force visited the battlefield. Members of the House Interior Committee made the tour while considering whether to empower the National Park Service to buy more land in the area. A bill to allow the park to expand never got out of the committee level in 1958, but Rep. John Foley resubmitted it for consideration in 1959. While describing the condition of the battlefield, the committee highlighted the church in its official report:

> Antietam now consists of only 183 acres. The holdings through the core of the battlefield are almost entirely confined to narrow strips bordering the park roads. Today a chrome and orange house trailer, complete with tall TV antenna, rests semi-permanently within fifty feet of the historic Dunker Church site. Tomorrow the ghostly cannonballs may be sailing through scores of living rooms in the Bloody Cornfield and along Bloody Lane.[3]

A September 13, 1959, editorial in the *Baltimore American* entitled "Antietam: Shrine or Gas Station," asked a series of pertinent questions:

> Would Pennsylvania let Valley Forge become a suburb of Philadelphia? Or, Little Round Top become a housing project? Would Virginia fill in the Crater at Petersburg, or Texas forget the Alamo? The answer, of course, is an emphatic "No." But would our own state let one of the most historic spots in America be hidden behind gas stations, refreshment stands, and housing developments? Anyone who has visited Antietam National Battlefield recently knows the answer to that one—of course it would. Unless the state of Maryland and the Federal Government, together or

---

2 *Morning* [Hagerstown] *Herald*, September 8, 1958.

3 John W. Stepp, "Task Force of House Weighs Antietam Field," Washington, D.C., *Evening* [Hagerstown] *Star*, April 11, 1959.

Even after the Dunker Church was rebuilt in 1962, the formidable problems faced by the National Park Service in restoring the grounds surrounding the church and the West Woods to their 1862 appearance were readily visible. *ANB*

separately, act immediately, one of the nation's most important Civil War battlefields will be lost to future generations.[4]

However, it was not until April 24, 1960, that President Dwight D. Eisenhower signed the bill permitting Antietam National Battlefield to purchase up to 600 additional acres, and to work out non-development agreements with the property holders of up to 1,200 more. An editorial in the *Washington Post* hailed the action:

Congress has always wanted the locale of the bloodiest battle in North America preserved, but in the past it has been willing to gamble on the patriotism of private citizens to purchase the battleground for the nation. At last it apparently sees the necessity for the investment of public funds in

4 "Antietam: Shrine or Gas Station?," *Baltimore American*, September 13, 1959.

this historic spot that will live in memory as long as the United States survives.[5]

This was all good news—more acreage of the battlefield could and would be preserved. But would that funding include the preservation of historic buildings? Visitors to Antietam continued to be touched by the plight of the Dunker Church. One visitor, John McDermott of South Salem, New York, went so far as to build a 60" x 36" replica of the building, which he presented to Superintendent Doust.[6]

Antietam staff again stepped up their efforts to help get the church rebuilt. In early 1960, Superintendent Doust directed Park Historian Robert Lagemann to prepare an extensive historic structures report on the Dunker Church. The report contained several thorough sections and, just as historian Tuckerman's report had nearly ten years previously, argued convincingly that the church should be rebuilt. Lagemann's report covered historical data, such as land ownership and the church's role in the battle, as well as architectural information and interpretive possibilities for the park.

Lagemann summarized his stance that rebuilding the Dunker Church is essential to Antietam National Battlefield with a passionate argument worth quoting extensively:

> In the official reports of nearly every commander in the northern part of the field the Dunker Church is referred to; Hooker's, Williams', Crawford's, Hood's, and Jackson's, just to cite a few. In nearly every account of the Battle of Antietam written since, the action around the Dunker Church is prominent, from the briefest summaries in textbooks to very detailed analyses. It is almost impossible to give a meaningful account of the battle without repeatedly referring to the Dunker Church: in explaining Lee's reasons for placing his lines where he did; in outlining the direction of and the immediate goal of Hooker's and Mansfield's attacks; of Hood's counterattack and the West Woods "ambush"; and many other prime elements of the battle and its aftermath. In interpreting the battle to visitors

---

5 Snell and Brown, *Antietam National Battlefield and National Cemetery, Sharpsburg, Maryland: An Administrative History*, 306-307; "Eisenhower Signs Antietam Park Bill," *Washington Post*, November 23, 1960.

6 *Daily* [Hagerstown] *Mail*, June 24, 1959.

on the field, not only are these basic elements of the battle narrated in their relationship to the Dunker Church, but the church itself is frequently pointed out as the central connecting point with which to orient other locations in the northern part of the field. The absence of the building is decidedly a handicap in attempting to thus acquaint the visitor with the inter-relationship of the individual actions which hinge on this location. With the absence of the church building with which to orient the distant parts of the field from which it was formerly visible, a distinct sense of loss is experienced daily by park visitors attempting to tie together the battle using the building as the focal point, as has been done in most of the written material with which they are informed on this battle. A restored Dunker Church would not only greatly facilitate interpretation of the Battle of Antietam for the visiting public, but would in itself be a deserving complement to the visible heritage of the United States.[7]

Because so many promising efforts had ended in failure, it seemed as if it would take a miracle to get the Dunker Church rebuilt—or at least some monumental event. Luckily, one was about to wash over the United States: the Civil War Centennial.

Large-scale plans were underway to commemorate the centennial of the war in many parts of the nation, and Maryland was no exception. The Washington County Committee for the Commemoration of the Centennial of the Battle of Antietam was formed in 1958, and had ambitious plans for the event. The group was headed by Dr. Walter Shealy, who served as its president, and included nine directors of specific committees. At its meeting in May of that year, the committee highlighted three projects it wanted to see completed before the centennial took place: (1) Restoration of the barn used by Clara Barton as a hospital; (2) A bypass to remove traffic from the Burnside Bridge, and; (3) The reconstruction of the Dunker Church.[8]

Concurrently, a "Citizens Committee," also known as the "Philadelphia Committee," met on March 31, 1960, with officials of the Department of the Interior, National Park Service, in Philadelphia, Pennsylvania. It was led by

---

7 Lagemann, Historic Structures Report for the *Dunkard Church, Antietam National Battlefield, May 25, 1960,* 51-54.

8 "Directors Named to Head Celebration: Centennial Group Favors Work on Restoration Jobs by1962," *Morning* [Hagerstown] *Herald,* May 6, 1958.

Page T. Otto of the Sharpsburg Rifles, a reinstated Civil War unit composed (strangely enough) of descendants of the original members of the Dunker Church. Otto and the rest of his group met in regional director's Ronald F. Lee's office with Lee, George A. Palmer, and staff and directors from the region. This was a preparatory meeting to discuss the possibility of reconstructing the Dunker Church on the battlefield. Rev. Austin Cooper, was present, representing the Brethren Historical Committee of the Church of the Brethren. The "Citizens Committee" presented its case forcefully and convincingly. After a long day of meetings, Lee and his directors gave a thumbs-up for the reconstruction of the historic church.

Writing to the members of the Brethren Historical Committee, Rev. Cooper proclaimed, "Brethren, we all feel that this has been a victory in many ways." It probably didn't hurt that Ronald F. Lee was a descendent of Confederate General Robert E. Lee, or that Page "Ted" Otto was the husband of Betty J. Otto (and later, historian at the battlefield park) and the great-grandson of Rev. John E. Otto, the last elder-minister of the Dunker Church. The chances of any of the proposed projects of the Washington County Historical Society being successfully implemented increased significantly with the addition of one more individual to the local Centennial planning: Maryland Governor Millard Tawes.[9]

The governor was a big supporter of the Centennial Commemoration and he saw it as an opportunity for Maryland to honor its history as well as gain national exposure. Tawes encouraged several special events in the state and personally participated in many of them. The governor delivered the keynote address at a Centennial planning dinner in Hagerstown on June 9, 1960. In front of a large crowd, Tawes declared his intentions to help make the Civil War Centennial in Washington County the "best it could be." He ended his speech by stating simply, "I am at your service."[10]

Governor Tawes backed up his words by including special funding in his state budget the following year to pay for the reconstruction of the

9   Report of Rev. H. Austin Cooper to the Brethren Historical Committee re: the March 31, 1960 meeting in Philadelphia, dated May 3, 1960; "Plans of Reconstruction," notes on the Philadelphia meeting made by Rev.Cooper, Austin Cooper Collection, BHLA, Elgin, IL.

10 Davis, *Completion Report—Reconstruction of Dunkard Church Building (Furnishings), Antietam National Battlefield Site, Sharpsburg, Maryland, November 30, 1962,* 12; "This County Well Ahead in Centennial Planning," *The Daily* [Hagerstown] *Mail,* November 2, 1959.

Dunker Church. On the 98th anniversary of the battle, September 17, 1960, the Maryland State Board of Public Works officially announced that $35,000 would be allocated to the National Park Service to rebuild the Dunker Church. Maryland would provide the money, and the NPS would provide the site, approach roads and parking, professionally prepared project plans, supervise the construction work, and operate and maintain the church after it was completed. The board announced that restoration of the church was more appropriate than spending the money on a monument or memorial of some sort on the site.[11]

News that the church would be rebuilt was greeted with widespread praise locally and across the nation. Many local groups and dignitaries applauded the move, as did the Civil War Centennial Commission. An editorial in the *Baltimore American* summed up the feelings of many:

> In announcing the program for rebuilding the church on the site of the original structure, the Civil War Centennial Commission pointed out that such a project is "highly desirable for historical and educational reasons." There can be no doubt about the truth of that statement. It is to be hoped that a committee, named to confer with Governor Tawes and representatives of the National Park Service will be able to work out a plan for restoring the old Dunker Church.[12]

After nearly forty years, the Dunker Church would return to take its place on the Antietam National Battlefield.

11 "Battle Church Restoral Set," *Washington Post*, September 18, 1960.

12 James C. Mullikin, "Civil War Centennial Group Lauded for Plan to Rebuild Antietam Church," *Baltimore American*, May 1, 1960.

Chapter 12

Completing the Task:
The Rededication of the Dunker Church

In February 1961, the National Park Service accepted a $35,000 donation from the state of Maryland for the specific purpose of reconstructing the Dunker Church.

Under the specified terms, the National Park Service would prepare the foundation and furnish the bricks, windows, doors, and shutters, as well as all other specialty millwork. Archie Franzen, Supervising Architect of Harpers Ferry National Monument, would supervise this work, as well as work done by the contractors. Elmer Boyer agreed to let Historian Robert Lagemann to see the Dunker Church materials, but he could not photograph or measure them. Understanding it would be difficult to make accurate copies without exact details, and knowing that the Maryland donation allowed them some financial flexibility, Park Service officials decided to simply purchase the materials from Boyer for $6,000. "We believe that inclusion of the original materials in the Dunker Church adds that touch of intimate association with an historical event and therefore justifies their acquisition," explained Franzen in the final report.[1]

---

1 Snell and Brown, Antietam *National Battlefield and National Cemetery, Sharpsburg, Maryland: An Administrative History*, 319-320; Davis, *Completion Report—Reconstruction of Dunkard Church Building*, 1-2.

The Dunker Church being rebuilt on its original foundation in 1961. *ANB*

On May 6, 1961, a groundbreaking service officially kicked off the reconstruction of the Dunker Church. Despite rainy conditions, more than 100 people attended the service. The bad weather shortened the otherwise historic event. Representatives of several groups involved in the rebuilding process used spades to overturn shovels of dirt within the original foundation of the church. Those participating included: Russell McClain, executive assistant to Maryland Governor Millard Tawes; Dr. Walter Shealy of the Washington County Historical Society; Rev. Austin Cooper of the Church of the Brethren; Page T. Otto of the Sharpsburg Rifles; Benjamin Davis, Superintendent of Antietam National Battlefield; Ronald F. Lee, and Evind T. Scoyen, Assistant Director of the National Park Service.[2]

The speaking parts of the ceremony were moved out of the rain and into the Sharpsburg Museum. In his speech commemorating the event, Scoyen offered the following:

Once again this small white church [will serve] as a point of orientation, this time for the visitor touring the battlefield. It will stand this time as a

2 *The Daily* [Hagerstown] *Mail*, May 8, 1961.

beacon to the people who will be searching to understand the deeper reasons and motives why our forefathers fought so valiantly, each for the cause he thought was just. There is meaning, too, in the fact that the church will rise, as it were, from its ruins, to claim once again its place on the scene. It can mean to us that that which is good and righteous will endure, no matter the storms that buffet it.[3]

During the process of planning the reconstruction, Franzen and Tuckerman contacted as many local citizens as possible familiar with the church—those who had either attended services there, or who had a special interest in the battle. Their testimony was "critically appraised and measured against those physical features, both apparent and implied, that can be seen from examining existing photographs." The two men also visited other historic Churches of the Brethren in the area to compare specific details, notably structures in Tilghmanton, Downsville, and Brownsville, Maryland, as well as Welsh Run, Pennsylvania.[4]

The original Dunker Church artifacts purchased from Elmer Boyer contained representative examples of the majority of the materials employed, such as joists, floorboards, and benches. Unfortunately, they did not include all the components in the quantity required for the complete reconstruction. This was not a surprise. Souvenir hunters had pilfered much from the wreckage of the church before Boyer was able to salvage what he had. The fabrication of additional pieces modeled on the originals, as well as repair to some original materials, was arranged through the monument shop facilities at Harpers Ferry. A Building Restoration Specialist named Robert Vorhees from the National Park Service was transferred in to perform the work.[5]

---

3 Snell and Brown, *Antietam National Battlefield and National Cemetery, Sharpsburg, Maryland: An Administrative History*, 320; address of Evind T. Scoyen, Assistant Director, National Park Service, on file in Antietam National Battlefield library.

4 Archie W. Franzen, *Historic Structures Report, Part 1 (Architectural Data Section), Prepared for the Reconstruction of the Dunkard Church, Antietam National Battlefield Site, October 31, 1960*, 1.

5 Davis, *Completion Report—Reconstruction of Dunkard Church*, 3; Archie W. Franzen, *Historic Structures Report, Part III, Reconstruction of Dunkard Church, Antietam National Battlefield Site, November 21, 1962*, 5.

A local brickyard named Cushwa and Sons out of Williamsport, Maryland, prepared satisfactory samples of handmade brick that matched the originals in size, color, and texture. An order was placed to produce 22,500 bricks to be used along with the approximately 3,000 original bricks Boyer had salvaged.[6]

On May 15, 1961, the working construction drawings were approved and bids advertised for with the opening date set for June 30. On the official invitation for bids form, the description of the work to be performed was described as follows:

> Reconstruction of the Dunker Church is to be a one-story brick masonry building built on the original footings, repaired as necessary. Roof framing to be wood truss with a wood shingle roof covering. Original woodwork to be used as available, Reproductions to be used elsewhere. Interior to be painted; exterior brickwork painted. Work to be completed in 180 calendar days.[7]

A problem with the type of shingles specified in the original description resulted in a new bidding process on July 20 so that submitting contractors could amend their prior bids. Five area contractors submitted bids ranging from $12,884 to $17,930. Hagerstown's Blake Company had the lowest bid and was selected for the project. A pre-construction conference on July 31 between representatives of the Blake Company and Superintendent Benjamin Davis and Architect Archie Franzen. Subcontractors for the Blake Company also included: Masonry, John R. Mitchell, Hagerstown; Truss fabricators, Cavetown Planing Mill, Cavetown, Maryland; Roofing, Bonded Applicators, Hagerstown; Plastering, Whitlock and Dusing, Waynesboro, PA; Electric heating, Hub City Electric, Hagerstown; and Painting, G. M. Gehr and Sons, Hagerstown.[8]

---

6 Davis, *Completion Report—Reconstruction of Dunkard Church Building*, 2.

7 Franzen, *Historic Structures Report, Part III*, 3-5; Snell and Brown, *Antietam National Battlefield and National Cemetery, Sharpsburg, Maryland: An Administrative History*, 320; "Invitation for Bids," (construction contract), June 12, 1961, Antietam National Battlefield Library.

8 Franzen, *Historic Structures Report, Part III*, 4-5.

Construction of the Dunker Church on the original site started on August 7, 1961. The masonry phase was completed by September 18. The original brick was piled around the entrance doors of the church. By October 5, the Blake Company had the structure under roof, and the plastering work finished on the 25th of that month. The window sashes were fitted by November 1, the shutters hung on the 15th, and the painting of the exterior of the building completed by the 29th.[9]

Floor installation began on December 7. Salvaged material made up only about 1/10 of what was required. To make up the difference, the National Park Service purchased new material of the same species from the Cavetown Planing Mill. The new boards were processed to duplicate the salvaged floor in width, thickness, and matching tongues and grooves. Following completion of the floor, the doors were hung on December 21. Painting on the interior of the building, as well as the trim, was completed by the end of the month. There were enough salvaged components to make ten long benches and one short bench, and fabrication of the remaining benches began in January. Only one leg of the Elder's [preacher's] table had been saved, so a new table was also fabricated. The National Park Service took final acceptance of the structure from the contractors on January 9, 1962. National Park Service staff continued working on the interior of the building and its furnishings throughout the spring.[10]

In what may have been a first, the final bill submitted by the Blake Company to the U. S. government was lower than the original bid because a section of metal lath was deemed unnecessary. The overall price was lowered by $107.00, bringing the total to $12,777.00. After adding on the salaries for the Restoration Specialists and the cost of the bricks, lumber, and other miscellaneous supplies, the total for the reconstruction of the Dunker Church came in at $20,046.90. It is worth noting that this was almost $15,000 less than the amount allocated from the state of Maryland, and far less than the $50,000 estimate that had stopped the project many years before.[11]

9   Davis, *Completion Report—Reconstruction of Dunkard Church Building*, 5.

10 Ibid., 6-8.

11 Ibid., 9; Franzen, *Historic Structures Report, Part III*, 6.

Ruth Otto became the first "official" visitor to the rebuilt Dunker Church in 1962 on her 70th birthday. Ruth was the daughter of the last minister of the Dunker Church, Elder John E. Otto. *ANB*

By the Fourth of July the Dunker Church was officially ready to be opened to visitors. Daily hours were set to run from 8:30 a.m. until 4:45 p.m. on weekdays, and from 9:45 a.m. — 5:45 p.m. on weekends. A park ranger-historian (likely Mr. Lagemann) was stationed at the church to answer questions and discuss its fascinating history.

The first official public visitor to the "new" Dunker Church was Miss Ruth Otto, whose father John had been the church's last full-time pastor. Her great-uncle was Samuel Mumma, who had donated the land where the church stood. Miss Otto had attended services in the Dunker Church as a child, and her visit to the new building was even more special because it took place on her seventieth birthday.[12]

The official rededication of the Dunker Church took place on September 2, 1962. Once again Mother Nature failed to cooperate and rained drenched everyone present. The dedication service was held on the lawn adjacent to the church and featured addresses by many dignitaries, including Maryland State Senator George E. Snyder, Dr. Walter Shealy of the Washington County Historical Society, Rev. Austin Cooper of the Church of the Brethren, Page T. Otto of the Sharpsburg Rifles, Benjamin Davis, Superintendent of Antietam National Battlefield, George Palmer, Regional

12 Snell and Brown, *Antietam National Battlefield and National Cemetery, Sharpsburg, Maryland: An Administrative History*, 348; "Reconstructed Dunker Church at Antietam Open to the Public," *The Daily* [Hagerstown] *Mail*, July 7, 1962; "First Visitor to 'New' Dunker Church," *Morning* [Hagerstown] *Herald*, July 12, 1962.

A faded newspaper image of dignitaries at the rededication of the Dunker Church on September 2, 1962. Governor Millard Tawes, the keynote speaker, is second from the right. *The Daily Mail*

Director of the National Park Service, F. R. Sanders, Chairman of the Antietam-South Mountain Centennial Association, and Maryland Governor Millard Tawes.

"In a field shrouded with smoke, the church was the only visible landmark," explained Tawes in his keynote address. "This Dunker Church," he continued:

> stood out as a beacon by which commanders took their direction and men found their way in the smoky chaos of battle. . . . And so, let us here today, in the spirit of the Brethren who built it more than a century ago, rededicate this building to the advancement of peace among men and among nations and to the brotherhood of all mankind. May it stand, as it did in war, as a beacon to guide men searching their way through the darkness. May it stand throughout all ages as a symbol of mercy, peace, and under-standing.[13]

13 'Dunker Church Rededicated Despite Inclement Weather," *The Daily* [Hagerstown] *Mail*, September 14, 1962; *The Dedication of the Reconstructed Dunker Church,*

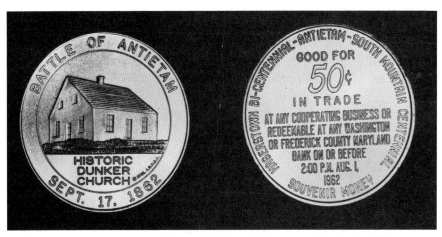

The commemorative coin issued for the Centennial observance of the Battle of Antietam, September 17, 1962. *ANB*

The second portion of the service was moved indoors to the Sharpsburg Community Hall. A religious service of commemoration followed, with representatives from more than thirty area churches. The service included a litany of dedication: "We hallow this ground and rededicate this church." The sermon was delivered by Dr. Harry Zeller, Jr., of California, whose great-great grandfather, Jacob Highbarger, had preached at the old Dunker Church and is buried in the Mumma cemetery. Despite the weather, a large crowd attended the ceremonies.[14]

The Dunker Church rededication kicked off two weeks of daily special events in Washington County to commemorate Antietam's centennial. There were several performances of "Hills of Glory," a large-scale dramatization of local history performed at Hagerstown's Municipal Stadium, as well as theme days dedicated to many local towns featuring special events in each community. A new monument on the battlefield was dedicated to Clara Barton. Ceremonies were held in recognition of the bicentennial of the founding of Hagerstown, and a grand two-day

September 2, 1962, 1:30 p.m., Antietam National Battlefield Site, Sharpsburg, Maryland.
Rededication program on file in park library.

14 Ibid.

re-enactment of the battle, the last that would take place on the actual battlefield, was also held.[15]

As was to be expected, the rebuilt Dunker Church played a key role throughout the extensive celebrations. The official logo and letterhead of the centennial featured a drawing of the church. A commemorative coin was minted with the church's image on it. The Washington County Historical Society at the Mansion House in Hagerstown City Park displayed the original Dunker Bible that had been returned from New York. The Sharpsburg Church of the Brethren featured an exhibit on Dunker history. And perhaps, in Nature's way of linking their significance, out of all the weeks of special events it only rained two days—for the Dunker Church rededication, and on the 100th battle anniversary itself.[16]

15 *Program for the Eighteen-Day Centennial Commemoration of the Battle of Antietam and Hagerstown, Maryland, Bicentennial, August 31 Through September 17, 1962*, ii-vii, xiv-xv, viii-xi, xvii-xxiii.

16 Official letterhead (logo) of the Antietam Centennial Celebration, *The Daily* [Hagerstown] *Mail*, October 14, 1958; "Centennial Planner Trying to Get Everyone Into the Act," *The Daily* [Hagerstown] *Mail*, November 25, 1961; "Antietam Centennial Commemorative Coin, 1962": http://americancivilwarrelics.com/Civil%20War%20Antietam.htm; "Dunker Church Bible Returned," *The Daily* [Hagerstown] *Mail*, August 30, 1962; "Dunker Church Members Plan to Open Exhibit to Public," *The Daily* [Hagerstown] *Mail*, August 29, 1962.

Chapter 13

The 125th and 150th Anniversaries
of the Battle of Antietam

The reconstructed Dunker Church on its original foundation, rededicated in 1962 for the centennial anniversary, became an integral part of Antietam National Battlefield, and perhaps the centerpiece to which all other sites on the battlefield could be oriented.

The little meetinghouse became a major part of the tour experience and pre-dated the Visitor Center, which did not open until 1963 (in a somewhat smaller version than it is today). In the 1980s, the park conducted a tree-planting program in the historic West Woods, restoring the Dunker Church area to its Civil War-era appearance. The church area is the first stop on the battlefield driving tour, and hosts ranger talks, living history presentations, medical, and music programs through much of the year. The church serves as a reference point for hikers, military staff rides, and public charity walks and races, and was even a checkpoint for the 1992 Tour DuPont bicycle race. The church is included, in one way or another, in most park special events, such as the Memorial Illumination and annual battle anniversary programs.

September 17, 1987, marked the 125th anniversary of the Battle of Antietam and the Bicentennial of the Constitution of the United States. The life of the Constitution and the Union it created were in deep jeopardy just 75 years after their creation when two mighty armies, North and South—Americans all—clashed along the banks of Antietam Creek near Sharpsburg, Maryland. As the program so eloquently observed:

As a result of the bloodshed at Antietam, our nation became a more perfect union and Lincoln's Emancipation Proclamation, which became incorporated as the Thirteenth Amendment to our Constitution, now guaranteed that neither slavery nor involuntary servitude shall ever again exist within the United States.

Richard J. Rambur, superintendent of Antietam National Battlefield in 1987, welcomed visitors to the park's commemoration from September 12-20. The official program of events included, for the visitor's convenience, the activities of "other groups" who were also conducting special commemorative programs in conjunction with the 125th anniversary:

In taking time to commemorate the people 'who, on this field, offered their lives in maintenance of their principles,' we can appreciate the supreme sacrifice given for our freedom. We can reflect upon the life of the Civil War soldier and civilian to appreciate the hardships and challenges of survival resulting from the battle.

We sincerely hope that your interest will continue in preserving the resources of our park.[1]

To mark the 125th anniversary, 500 commemorative medals were produced with the U.S. Constitution on one side (because its 200th birthday was the same day as the battle), and "Antietam" on the other. The medals were sold at the battlefield for $10 each."[2]

The planned events at the battlefield spanned the gamut from interpretive programs by park staff and lectures by noted Civil War historians, to rifle and cannon firing demonstrations and walking tours of the battlefield including torchlight evening tours. Musical programs, military displays, and special anniversary ceremonies rounded out the special commemorations.

Noted Civil War historians delivered lectures, including Gary Gallagher, Ted Alexander, Ed Bearss, Perry Jamieson, Dennis Frye,

---

1   *125th Anniversary, Battle of Antietam Program of Events, September 12-27, 1987.*

2   Charles Hillinger, Charles Hillinger's America, "Marking 125th Anniversary of Antietam Battle," *Los Angeles Times*, September 20, 1987. http://articles.latimes.com/1987-09-20/news/vw-9238_1_125th-anniversary/2.

William Potter, Rev. John Schildt, John Michael Priest, Vince Armstrong, and Jay Luvass, among others. Special Civil War musical programs were offered daily by Jim Morgan, John Priest, Colleen Mastrangelo, and others.

During the early afternoon on Thursday, September 17, 23,100 red, white, and blue balloons representing the casualties at Antietam were released in the National Cemetery by children from 25 county schools. The formal opening ceremony for the 125th anniversary followed with Rev. John Schildt speaking in the National Cemetery where the Shepherd College Band also performed.

On Saturday, September 19, the 125th Anniversary Parade kicked off on Main Street in Sharpsburg. The closing ceremony held at the Visitor Center was led by Jay Luvass of the U. S. Army War College on the afternoon of Sunday, September 20, where a military band performed.

The overall 125th anniversary commemorations concluded on Saturday and Sunday, September 26-27, with day-long events and a reenactment of the battle on the 27th on private property near Boonsboro, Maryland. Some 2,000 Civil War buffs from 41 states participated in the dramatic event, which was sponsored by The American Civil War Commemorative Committee (ACWCC).

Events scheduled at the Dunker Church included an "Old Tyme Service" conducted by the Sharpsburg Church of the Brethren on the afternoon of Sunday, September 13, and programs on "Civil War Medicine" by Drs. Wheat and Hinks on Saturday and Sunday, September 19-20. A non-denominational worship service was held in the church from 10:00 -11:00 a.m. on Sunday, September 20.[3]

By way of contrast and comparison, the 2012 Sesquicentennial marking the 150th anniversary of the battle was held from September 14-17 at Antietam National Battlefield. Superintendent Susan Trail welcomed visitors on behalf of the park staff and called the 150th anniversary a "watershed event" for "one of the best preserved Civil War battlefields in the country."

The theme "HOPE for freedom" was emphasized throughout the event, which noted that Geneal Lee's retreat that ended his first invasion of the

---

3 *125th Anniversary, Battle of Antietam Program of Events, September 12-27, 1987*; Hillinger, "Marking 125th Anniversary of Antietam Battle," *Los Angeles Times*, September 20, 1987.

An annual Brethren commemorative worship service in the rebuilt Dunker Church. Rev. Austin Cooper who started the worship service in 1970 is sitting at the end of the preachers' table in the foreground. *ANB and BHLA*

North enabled President Abraham Lincoln to issue the preliminary Emancipation Proclamation, which gave the Civil War the "dual purposes of preserving the Union and ending slavery." The nation would eventually be saved, but at the cost of some 700,000 dead and many hundreds of thousands of wounded. The war freed about four million slaves. The Battle of Antietam changed the course of our history.

The Sesquicentennial program included a park-wide shuttle bus that ran every 10-15 minutes between the Visitor Center and park tour stops, an inter-event shuttle bus, a "Company Street," and special programs and exhibits at the Newcomer and Pry Houses on the battlefield. The Newcomer House served as the welcome center for Maryland's "Heart of the Civil War Heritage Area" exhibits, while the Pry House Field Hospital Museum offered special programs throughout the weekend. The states of Pennsylvania and Virginia provided mobile exhibits highlighting their participation in the battle and the war, and C-SPAN operated an educational

The Sesquicentennial emblem in 2012 showing the Dunker Church. *ANB*

bus. The usual first aid and concessions tents were set up, and the Western Maryland Interpretive Association, a non-profit partner of Antietam National Battlefield, operated the Antietam Museum Store offering new books by Drs. Thomas Clemens and Bradley Gottfried, and two new park brochures on the West Woods and the role of artillery in the battle, respectively. For something truly unique, certified National Park Service "Antietam Battlefield Guides" could be reserved for a special two- and one-half hour general tour of the expansive battlefield, or for a tightly customized program of any length for all interest levels, ages and group sizes.[4]

---

4   Thomas J. Clemens, ed., Ezra Carman, *The Maryland Campaign of 1862*, 3. vols. (Savas Beatie, 2010-2017), and Bradley M. Gottfried, *The Maps of Antietam: An Atlas of*

The opening program of the four-day observance was held Friday, September 14 at 10:00 a.m., and the 150th Commemorative Ceremony took place Monday, September 17 from 12:30 - 2:00 p.m. on the main stage near the Maryland monument across the Hagerstown Pike (Dunker Church Road) from the church. At 3:00 p.m. on the 17th, a "Remembrance of the Fallen" ceremony in the National Cemetery featured a reading of the names of all the documented soldiers from both armies killed/mortally wounded in the battle. (The Confederate dead, of course, are not buried in the National Cemetery.) A closing program followed in the National Cemetery at 7:00 p.m.

The Inter-Event Shuttle ran every 10-15 minutes between the parking area of the Washington County Agricultural Education Center north of the battlefield, the Visitor Center at the battlefield park, the Sharpsburg Heritage Festival downtown, and the Sesquicentennial Antietam-Sharpsburg re-enactment off Route 65 northwest of the battlefield.

At the Visitor Center, those attending the events had the option of watching a 30-minute documentary on Antietam that played twice an hour, as well as check out the well-stocked bookstore and various relics and displays. "Company Street," in front of the Visitor Center, included a family and youth tent featuring hands-on activities for all ages, a photography exhibit featuring Alexander Gardner's iconic battlefield images of Antietam, an emancipation exhibit, food vendors, and the important speaker's tent where notable scholars of the Maryland Campaign of 1862 and the Battle of Antietam spoke throughout the four-day event.

A partial listing of scholars who spoke in the Speaker's Tent and elsewhere on the field included Stephen Potter, Stephen Recker, Bob O'Connor, Benjamin Franklin Cooling, Drew Gilpin Faust, Ed Bearss, Perry Jamieson, James I. Robertson, Tom Clemens, Dwight Pitcaithley, Kathleen Ernst, Mark Neely, James McPherson, Ted Alexander, Alann Schmidt, Nick Picerno, and Civil War artist Mort Kunstler. The Maryland Historical Society Players, Fort McHenry Fife and Drum Corps, and the Wildcat Regimental Band provided outstanding music during the Sesquicentennial.

"The Pennsylvania Civil War 150 Road Show" and "Virginia Civil War 150 History Mobile" 53-foot expandable tractor-trailers, featured interactive state-of-the-art museum-quality sight and sound exhibits detailing the

---

the Antietam (Sharpsburg) Campaign, including the Battle of South Mountain, September 2 - 20, 1862 (Savas Beatie, 2012).

Park Ranger Alann Schmidt standing next to the interpretive signage for the Dunker Church. *Alann Schmidt*

experiences of the men, women, and children from Pennsylvania and Virginia during the Civil War. These mobile units were parked in the grassy area between the Visitor Center and the Hagerstown Pike (Dunker Church Road). C-SPAN's American History Exhibit was also located there.

Battlefield tour stops featuring talks by park rangers and living history buffs included the Dunker Church, the North Woods/Poffenberger Farm, the Cornfield, the Mumma and Roulette Farms, the Sunken Road, and Burnside Bridge. The usual weapons and artillery firing demonstrations were held daily throughout the commemoration. At the Dunker Church, Park Ranger Alann Schmidt delivered 30-minute lectures on the church during the mornings and afternoons entitled "Beacon of Peace."

A highlight of the entire 150th anniversary observance was the Forever postage stamp of the Battle of Antietam issued by the U. S. Postal Service. The color painting selected is by Thure de Thulstrup and depicts the Union charge of Colonel William H. Irwin's brigade toward the Dunker Church. The First Day Cover stamped envelope with the first day of issue postmark

First Day Cover with commemorative stamp issued by the U. S. Postal Service
on September 17, 2012, for the 150th anniversary observance of the battle.
Dr. Jeff Bach

for September 17, 2012 (Sesquicentennial Station, Sharpsburg, MD 21782),
also includes a postmark stamp featuring the Dunker Church.[5]

Other program events were held September 18-22 featuring park
historian Ted Alexander, Mark Snell, Thomas McGrath, Alann Schmidt,
and Bob Zeller. Finally, Robert Stanton, David Blight, and "living
historians" portraying the 54th Massachusetts participated in a special 2:00
p.m. ceremony on the 22nd entitled "Free at Last: A Proclamation,"
highlighting the "HOPE for freedom" theme that grew from the carnage of
Antietam.[6]

---

5   The Antietam Forever Stamp: http://about.usps.com/news/national-releases/2012/ pr12
047.htm; https://store.usps.com/store/browse/productDetailSingleSku.jsp?productId=P
842394&categoryId=stamp-gifts.

6   Antietam National Battlefield, *150th Anniversary of the Battle of Antietam*, Event
Program, September 14-17, 2012.

"I Speak to Those Who Listen"

As strange as this may sound, if it hadn't been for the Battle of Antietam, the Mumma Church probably would have remained in obscurity save for its divine service as a House of the Lord for the Brethren. Had there been no battle at Sharpsburg, the Mumma Church would have almost certainly grown and prospered until it possibly rivaled the Manor Church in size and influence. Additions would likely have been made to the building. The district Brethren leadership may have allowed it to break away from The Manor and begin its own program of preaching and missionary activities in the area. Had it not been for this terrible battle, the world may never have heard of the Dunker Church.

The Mumma Church—after the battle forever after known as the Dunker Church—is one of the most iconic battlefield structures of the entire American Civil War. Thanks to Alexander Gardner's horrific images of the little church and its surroundings, taken just two days after the battle, anyone even remotely interested in the Civil War in general, and this battle in particular, will recall seeing the humble, damaged, and unassuming structure with Confederate dead littering the foreground.

Every year, some 330,000 visitors come to visit Antietam National Battlefield. While this number is far fewer than those who visit Gettysburg each year, everyone who comes to the Visitor Center sets eyes on the reconstructed Dunker Church across the way, and probably drive past it on even the most cursory tour of the battlefield. Most, however, take the time to visit the church, read the interpretive signs outside, and step inside to marvel

The Dunker Church today, showing the two-color paint scheme on the doors. *Alann Schmidt*

at the simplicity of it all. "Simplify, Simplify," admonished Henry David Thoreau in *Walden*. Thoreau would have thoroughly approved of the humbleness of the Dunker Church, which was much like his own little house at Walden Pond.[1]

As described earlier, the Dunker Church served initially as a first aid station for wounded Confederates and then as a temporary hospital—a sort of triage center—offering immediate medical care for soldiers of both armies. Untold numbers of amputations were performed within its walls, a morgue was set up, bodies were embalmed, and the church grounds served as a temporary small cemetery. General Thomas J. "Stonewall" Jackson, Clara Barton, and even President Abraham Lincoln, among other notables, are associated with the church.

As unlikely as it sounds today, the bloodiest day in American history swirled around a humble whitewashed church dedicated to peaceful nonviolence, equality, and the brotherhood of all men. The irony of the

---

1 Henry David Thoreau and Stephen Fender, *Walden* (Oxford and New York, 2008).

The Memorial Illumination at Antietam National Battlefield—23,000 candles represent one for every soldier killed, wounded, or missing at the September 17, 1862, battle. *ANB*

Dunker Church being surrounded and inundated by so much bloodshed was not lost on many of the leaders who participated in the battle. The Dunkers were pacifists who believed violence and participation in war was a sin. As the Commandment reads, "Thou shall not kill." The battle shook to the very core the Dunker's dream of a peaceful world where everyone lived in harmony.

The Dunker Church served both as a beacon of peace and a beacon of hope. Everyone was welcome within its walls to give thanks and to praise the Lord. Inside, people could find peace and harmony and refuge from the storms of life. During the battle, wounded soldiers of both sides sought refuge there.

The decision to repair and restore the iconic Dunker Church after the battle was almost a foregone conclusion. Samuel Mumma, who had originally donated the land for the religious building, decided after the battle ended that the church should stand "as a symbol of peace and goodwill among men of all creeds and differences." Elder Daniel P. Sayler informed the Brethren, who were attending the meeting to decide whether or not to rebuild the church, that the battle damage to the church should be repaired and restored and that worship services should be resumed as soon as possible.[2]

For the people who call themselves Brethren, the Dunker Church stands as "an eternal symbol of peace on the site of the bloodiest single-day battle of the Civil War." The Brethren uphold the little battlefield church as "a symbol of tolerance, love, brotherhood, and service—a witness to the mind and spirit of Him whom we seek to serve."[3]

As recently as July 12, 2016, *Newsline*, the online newsletter of the Church of the Brethren, published a statement from its leaders about the recent violence and racial unrest around the country. These leaders cited the Dunker Church of Antietam Battlefield as a symbol of the calling of the Brethren to be a "landmark of refuge during a time of violence." The article included an image of the Dunker Church on the battlefield:

> In this season of escalating violence, the Brethren can again be a landmark of refuge like the simple bright walls of the Dunker meeting house on the Antietam battle field. It is not enough to add a hashtag or post an article on Facebook. We must return to the Scriptures that inform us about our work of caring for those who would be starved, stripped naked, and imprisoned. We must identify with the widow, the orphan, and the foreigner to our society. The Scriptures reminded earlier Christians of the historical and cultural forces that had defined and divided them as Jew, Gentile, slave, and master. Today, we need to be disciples who are able to recognize how deeply the powers and principalities of racial injustice have wounded our country—spiritually and physically. We need to understand what keeps us locked in this cycle of violence and we must search our souls for what it means to turn the other cheek, to go the extra mile, and to wash the feet of others.[4]

---

2   Cooper, "Upon This Rock—Build," 14.

3   Cooper and Scrogum, "The Dunker Church and the Church of the Brethren"; "40th Annual Dunker Church Worship Service, September 19, 2010, Antietam National Battlefield Park, Sharpsburg, Maryland…"

4   Carol A. Scheppard, Samuel Sarpiya, and Dale E. Minnich, "When Lamentations Are Not Enough: A Statement for the Church of the Brethren," *Newsline*, Church of the Brethren online, July 12, 2016, http://www.brethren.org/news/2016/church-leaders-call-brethren-to-be-refuge-during-violence.html.

E. Russell Hicks of the Church of the Brethren, a leading Washington County historian, wrote poetically about the Dunker Church:

I still exist as the little white church of the Antietam Battlefield. I live in the hearts of all who ever knew me. I am still a symbol of peace and brotherhood. Antietam was the battle that emancipated the slaves; I am a symbol of spiritual emancipation. . . . I represent unity . . . the Brotherhood of Man under the Fatherhood of a loving, kind God.[5]

Rev. Newton L. Poling of the Church of the Brethren addressed a group in Hagerstown, Maryland, in 1992. "Speaking as a descendant of the old Dunkers, let me say that if the Mumma Church at Antietam has served since 1862 to bring attention to the horror of war," he observed, "it has served a useful purpose, one that is close to the hearts of the Dunkers themselves—to renounce war and work for peace."[6]

Mary Sue Rosenberger reminds us poetically in her "Conversation at Antietam" of the inspirational power of the Dunker Church of Antietam Battlefield. An excerpt from her poem reads as follows:

Little Dunker meetinghouse, so peaceful and serene. How I wish that you could speak of what you've heard and seen. Wondering brought me here inside your walls that, whitewashed, glisten. The silence here speaks loud to me, "I speak to those who listen."

Then speak to me, small sentinel...

"I still hear the screams of men and beasts. Smell cannon smoke and blood. Feel the shells that broke my walls, and grieve that senseless flood. I had a glimpse of hell that day and tremble still in terror at the awful price of human pride, stubbornness and error."

So now, deserted meetinghouse, from what you've seen and heard, what wisdom would you share with us. Oh, speak to us your word.

---

5   Schildt, *Drums Along the Antietam*, 294-295.

6   Poling, "The Dunkers: Their Customs and Life Style in the Antietam Valley."

"The Dunkers said it long ago and its truth continues still: All war is sin and goes against God's gracious sovereign will."[7]

It is appropriate to allow Maryland Governor Millard Tawes the last word, for he is the one individual most responsible for accomplishing the reconstruction of the Dunker Church on the Antietam battlefield:

> And so, let us here today in the spirit of the Brethren who built it more than a century ago, rededicate this building to the advancement of peace among men and among nations and to the brotherhood of all mankind. May it stand, as it did in war, as a beacon to guide men searching their way through the darkness. May it stand throughout all ages as a symbol of mercy, peace, and understanding.[8]

7   Mary Sue Rosenberger, "Conversation at Antietam," Church of the Brethren *Messenger* (November 2010), 9.

8   "Dunker Church Rededicated Despite Inclement Weather," Hagerstown *The Daily Mail*, September 14, 1962. The text of Governor Tawes' speech is on file in the park library archives.

Antietam's Dunker Church:
A Tactical Overview

by Ted Alexander

If you were able to stand on the front steps of the Dunker Church on the afternoon of September 16, 1862, you would have looked across the adjacent Hagerstown Pike at fields full of grazing horses and hundreds of grayclad cavalrymen—horsemen of Brigadier General Fitzhugh Lee's brigade—lounging about smoking pipes, eating, reading letters from home or maybe napping.

Sharing the fields with the cavalry was the famous Texas Brigade, whose men were both lean and mean. Except for a half-ration of beef and green corn, the Lone Star soldiers had gone for three days without food prior to arriving at Sharpsburg. They were waiting there because of the promised their rations would arrive soon via supply wagon.

As the men in gray and butternut waited, firsthand accounts tell us that both cavalry commander Major General James Ewell Brown ("Jeb") Stuart and infantry division commander Brigadier General John Bell Hood were at the Dunker Church. Although it tends to be an overused term in Civil War narratives, these two commanders used the whitewashed house of worship as a temporary "headquarters." In his official after-action battle report, Hood erroneously referred to the modest structure as "Saint Mummas Church."

It was there at the church that these two generals received messages from videttes that Union columns were crossing Antietam Creek at the Hitt or "Upper Bridge" and at the Pry Ford. Stuart dispatched Fitz Lee's troopers and Hood sent elements of his infantry division down the Smoketown Road to the East Woods and beyond. Before long, infantry from Major General Daniel H. Hill's division, together with various artillery batteries, arrived in the vicinity of the church.

Late that afternoon and into dusk, the Confederates sparred with advance elements of Union Major General George B. McClellan's Army of the Potomac. The Union advance was composed of Major General George G. Meade's division of the First Corps. Among its regiments was the 13th Pennsylvania Reserve, better known as the "Pennsylvania Bucktails." This unit would earn glory on many battlefields of the war. Although the soldiers exchanged small arms and artillery fire for several hours in the vicinity of the East Woods and Miller's Cornfield, losses were light on both sides.

While some of Hood's men were so engaged, Major General Thomas J. "Stonewall" Jackson arrived on the field with a pair of divisions—his former division, now led by Brigadier General John R. Jones, and another under Brigadier Alexander R. Lawton. Both commands marched past the Dunker Church and deployed to the north and west along Hagerstown Pike. Jackson directed that two brigades—Lawton's former brigade of Georgians now under Colonel Marcellus Douglass, and old Isaac Trimble's outfit now under Colonel James A. Walker—be held in reserve near the church. As these troops were taking position, Stuart's cavalry fell back from the ensuing action and rested for a time in the fields east of the church.

Darkness brought an end to most of the firing in this sector. However, around 9:00 p.m. a 24-man scouting party from the 5th Pennsylvania Reserves moved from the East Woods and encountered elements of the 4th Alabama and 6th North Carolina. In the brief exchange of gunfire, Lieutenant H. P. Petriken, commander of the scouting party, fell mortally wounded and was left on the field to the mercy of the Confederates. Members from the 4th Alabama carried the wounded officer back to the church, where he was humanely cared for until he died later that night.

Around 10:00 p.m., General Hood received permission from Jackson to move his division about 200 yards behind the church so his men could rest and cook the promised rations ostensibly on the way. After positioning his troops, Hood rode out to assure the food was indeed on its way.

About dawn the next day, September 17, 1862, all hell broke loose in the fields and woodlots around the Dunker Church. The structure in and of itself was of little tactical value. From the start of the battle, however, it was recognized as a focal point of Union attacks in that sector. Indeed, Union First Corps commander Major General Joseph Hooker understood the importance of the small white church as a beacon because of the high ground upon which it sat. To seize this ground and penetrate the enemy front here would potentially break the hinge of the Confederate left flank held by Jackson's under-strength commands. Accordingly, Brigadier General Abner Doubleday's First Division of the First Corps was ordered to attack directly against the church. Doubleday's assault almost made it there, but was repulsed by the fierce resistance of Jackson's men. This fighting concentrated the combat onto the "Cornfield" and East Woods several hundred yards from the church. The action in these locations was some of the heaviest of the battle and proved deadly for the soldiers in the ranks and the officers who commanded them. In one counterattack, Confederate Brigadier General William Starke, leading his Louisiana brigade into the fight, was felled with three bullets in him. He was hauled to the vicinity of the church, where he expired about an hour later.

As Jackson's lines began to collapse in the face of overwhelming Union pressure, he sought reinforcements to hold his front. Among them was Hood's division, including the legendary Texas Brigade. As earlier noted, Jackson had given permission to Hood for his men to move behind the Dunker Church to rest and cook and eat their expected rations. The anticipated chow arrived late and consisted only of flour and bacon. They were in the middle of fixing their breakfast when Jackson called upon them. Going for three days without hot food was one thing. Being called up into battle and thus forced to leave their one hot meal angered many hundreds of Texans. "I have never seen a more disgusted bunch of boys and mad as hornets," recorded a Rebel officer.

Perhaps their anger gave them an edge in the combat that followed. The Texans, along with the rest of Hood's division, formed for battle across the road from the church. By 7:20 a.m. Hood's 2,000-man force moved out, stepping over the dead, wounded, and other debris of that morning's carnage and into one of the most famous attacks of the Civil War. The 1st Texas Infantry advanced the farthest, suffering 186 killed, wounded, and missing

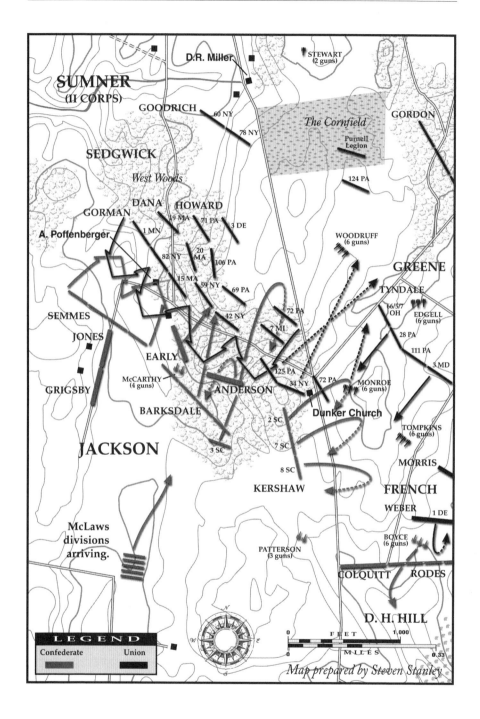

STEWART
(2 guns)

D.R. Miller

SUMNER
(II CORPS)

GOODRICH

60 NY

78 NY

The Cornfield

GORDON

Purnell
Legion

SEDGWICK

West Woods

124 PA

DANA   HOWARD

GORMAN
49 MA   71 PA   3 DE

A. Poffenberger

1 MN

WOODRUFF
(6 guns)

GREENE

82 NY   20
MA   106 PA

TYNDALE

15 MA   59 NY   69 PA

66/5/7
OH

EDGELL
(6 guns)

42 NY

72 PA

28 PA

SEMMES

7 MI

111 PA

JONES

3 MD

EARLY

125 PA

McCARTHY
(4 guns)

34 NY   72 PA

MONROE
(6 guns)

GRIGSBY

ANDERSON

Dunker Church

BARKSDALE

2 SC

TOMPKINS
(6 guns)

JACKSON

3 SC

7 SC

MORRIS

8 SC

FRENCH

KERSHAW

WEBER

1 DE

McLaws
divisions
arriving.

BOYCE
(6 guns)

PATTERSON
(3 guns)

COLQUITT   RODES

D. H. HILL

LEGEND

Confederate   Union

FEET   1,000

MILES

0.33

Map prepared by Steven Stanley

The Union advance on the Dunker Church and West Woods in the last major fighting around the church. This 1887 painting by Thure de Thulstrup was used for the 150th anniversary commemorative stamp of Antietam issued by the U. S. Postal Service. *LOC*

out of just 226 engaged—a staggering casualty rate of 82.3 percent. Many consider it the highest casualty rate suffered by any unit, North or South, in a one-day battle during the entire war.

One of the bloodiest affairs around the church and during the Battle of Antietam was the so-called "West Woods Massacre," which unfolded about 9:00 a.m. By that time, Jackson's veterans were limping off the field as individuals and in groups. The attacks of two Union Corps, the First and Twelfth, had spent themselves. However, thousands more Union soldiers were marching into the storm of combat.

Major General John Sedgwick's Second Division of the Union Second Corps was rapidly moving toward the Dunker Church and West Woods. Leading them was corps commander Major General Edwin V. Sumner. Unbeknownst to Sumner, Confederate divisions under Major General Lafayette McLaws and Brigadier General John Walker were arriving at the same time, and they were on a collision course with Sedgwick's left flank. This human Confederate tidal wave numbered more than 5,000 soldiers and, coupled with the arrival of more than 900 men of Brigadier General Jubal Early's brigade, was about to wash over Sedgwick's unwitting Unionists.

Before striking Sedgwick's division, however, the Confederates struck the raw recruits of the 125th Pennsylvania. A confused order had sent this Twelfth Corps unit into the West Woods right behind the Dunker Church. There, it was overwhelmed and driven back across Hagerstown Pike, losing 229 out of about 700 engaged.

With the Keystone soldiers out of the way, the Confederate attack struck Sedgwick's 5,437-man division. In about 20 minutes of hard fighting, 373 Union soldiers were killed outright, some from friendly fire; 1,593 more were wounded, many mortally; 244 men were later reported missing in action, a total of 2,210 or 40 percent of those engaged.

While the "West Woods Massacre" was taking place, the Second Division of the Union Twelfth Corps deployed in the swale between the Mumma farm and the Dunker Church. This 1,700-man command belonged to 61-year-old Brigadier General George Sears Greene. About 9:45 a.m., as the Confederates moved to flank Sedgwick, three South Carolina regiments from Brigadier General Joseph Kershaw's brigade diverted to the right and attacked the Union artillery fighting with Greene's division. This forlorn hope, which consumed less than 15 minutes, cost Kershaw about half his men. The South Carolinians withdrew behind the church.

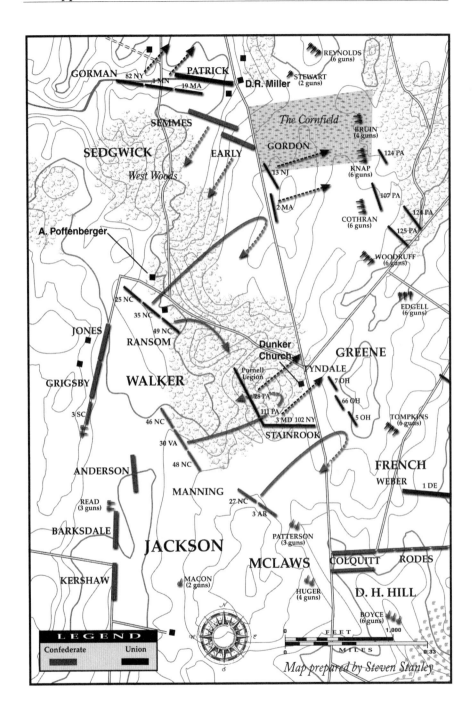

Map prepared by Steven Stanley

Next came three regiments from Confederate Colonel Van H. Manning's brigade. Once again the attacking Rebels were met with a devastating storm of canister and musketry from Greene's Yankees. "We were all cut to pieces," recalled a member of the 48th North Carolina. As one Ohio soldier observed, "They fell like grass before the mower." Manning, who fell wounded, carried around 1,400 soldiers into the fight and left 505 of them on the field killed, wounded and missing, all within a matter of minutes.

By 10:30 a.m. Greene held the Dunker Church and the area around it. Although reinforced by two more Twelfth Corps units and additional artillery, his men were exhausted from the morning's heavy combat and seriously low on ammunition. No further support arrived, and increased Confederate pressure threatened his flanks. Out of options, Greene withdrew to the East Woods around 12:30 p.m. His command had advanced farther and remained in action longer than any other Union division that day. In the process, he lost 552 men killed, wounded, and missing, or 31 percent of those engaged.

Although the major combat at Antietam thereafter shifted south to the Sunken Road (also known as the Bloody Lane) and later the Lower Bridge ("Burnside Bridge"), there was still more fighting to take place around the Dunker Church. As the Confederate lines buckled and then broke along the Sunken Road, Major General James Longstreet sought any available troops in the area to stem the relentless Union attacks. He ordered Colonel John R. Cook to lead an assault against the Union right flank attacking the Sunken Road. This demi-brigade, about 950 strong, consisted of the 3rd Arkansas, 27th North Carolina, and remnants of Tom Cobb's brigade. Cook formed for the attack just south of the Dunker Church. Once more yet another Confederate attack was driven back with heavy losses. By the time it was done, Cook suffered more than 50 percent casualties.

The final combat around the Dunker Church occurred around 2:00 p.m. Colonel William Irwin's Union brigade of the Second Division, Sixth Corps, had arrived on the field. Deploying from the Mumma farm, the brigade made a direct attack against the Confederate lines aroud the church. Part of Irwin's brigade made it to the church itself, but the Confederates had been reinforced with both infantry and artillery and blasted apart the Federal assault. More than 300 men were lost in this ill-advised and unsupported attack.

When all was said and done, more than 15,000 Union and Confederate soldiers fought around the Dunker Church that bloody day of September 17,

1862. Thousands were killed, wounded, or captured there. Their sacrifices were a major factor in making the church not only a battlefield shrine, but a national one as well. And they deserve to be remembered.

*   *   *

Ted Alexander, the former chief historian for Antietam National Battlefield, is widely recognized as one of the battle's leading authorities. He has published widely on this and other Civil War topics.

Sources used to prepare this appendix include:

The War of the Rebellion: A Compilation of the Official Records of the Union and Confederate Armies, 128 vols. (Washington, DC, 1880-1901), Series 1, vol. 19, pt. 1.

Alexander, Ted. *The Battle of Antietam: The Bloodiest Day* (Charleston, SC: The History Press, 2011).

————. "Forgotten Valor: Off the Beaten Path at Antietam." *Blue & Gray Magazine* : *Special Reprint, A Visitors Guide* (Columbus, OH: Blue & Gray Enterprises, 2002).

Armstrong, Marion V., Jr. *Opposing the Second Corps at Antietam: The Fight for the Confederate Left and Center on America's Bloodiest Day* (Tuscaloosa, AL: University of Alabama Press, 2016).

Carman, Ezra A., Thomas G. Clemens, ed. *The Maryland Campaign of September 1862.* vol. 2: *Antietam*. (El Dorado Hills, CA: Savas Beatie, 2012).

Simpson, Harold B. *Hood's Texas Brigade: Lee's Grenadier Guard.* (Waco, TX: Texian Press, 1970.)

Bibliography

Manuscripts

Antietam National Battlefield, Sharpsburg, Maryland.

Antietam Celebration Commission Invitation to President Franklin D. Roosevelt to speak at the 75th Anniversary of the Battle of Antietam, September 17, 1937.

Davis, Benjamin H. *Completion Report, Reconstruction of Dunkard Church Building (Furnishings), Antietam National Battlefield Site, Sharpsburg, Maryland, November 30, 1962.*

Franzen, Archie W. *Historic Structures Report, Part I (Architectural Data Section), Prepared for the Reconstruction of the Dunkard Church, Antietam National Battlefield Site, October 31, 1960.*

——. *Completion Report, Part III, Reconstruction of Dunkard Church, November 21, 1962.*

Lagemann, Robert L. *Historic Structures Report for the Dunkard Church, Antietam National Battlefield Site, May 25, 1960.*

——. *Historic Structures Report, Part 1, Furnishing Plan for the Dunkard Church, January 1962.*

1934 Scrapbook Files.

Snell, Charles W. and Sharon A. Brown. *Antietam National Battlefield and National Cemetery: An Administrative History.* Washington, D.C.: Department of the Interior, National Park Service, 1986.

Tuckerman, Louis E. *Report of the Old Dunkard Church and Site at Antietam National Battlefield Site, Sharpsburg, Maryland, August 1951.*

——. "Dunkard Church Property," August 1, 1951.

Brethren Historical Library and Archives
(Church of the Brethren General Offices, Elgin, Illinois)

Brethren Historical Committee Papers
Rev. H. Austin Cooper Collection
John T. Lewis File
Photographic Collection

Digitized Brethren Periodicals:

Brethren Digital Project online at https://archive.org/details/brethrendigital archives.
The Brethren Evangelist, November 17, 1951
The Gospel Messenger, September 1, 1906; February 2, 9, 16, 1952
The Gospel-Visitor, September 1863; March 1864
Inglenook, May 1, 1906
Messenger, October 1985; November 2010

Libraries, Archives and Special Collections

Alderman Library, University of Virginia, Charlottesville
Leyburn Library, Washington and Lee University, Lexington, Virginia
Preston Library, Virginia Military Institute, Lexington
Washington County Historical Society, Hagerstown, Maryland
Washington County Land Records, County Courthouse, Hagerstown, Maryland

Newspapers

Baltimore American, September 13, 1959; May 1, 1960
Cincinnati Daily Gazette, September 21, 1867
Hagerstown, MD: *The Daily Mail*, June 10, 1959; June 24, 1959; November 2, 1959; May 8, 1961; July 7, 1962; July 12, 1962; July 30, 1962; September 14, 1962
Hagerstown, MD: *The Morning Herald*, March 3, 1937; April 3, 1937; January 28, 1951; April 18, 1958; May 6, 1958; September 8, 1958; July 12, 1962
Washington, D.C.: *Evening Star*, April 11, 1959
Washington Post, September 18, 1960; November 23, 1960
Washington Times and online, June 18, 2004
Winchester, VA: *Evening Star*, May 1, 1951

Selected Books, Booklets, and Articles

Alexander, Ted. *The Battle of Antietam: The Bloodiest Day*. Charleston, SC: History Press, 2011.

———. "Forgotten Valor: Off the Beaten Path at Antietam." *Blue & Gray Magazine* – Special Reprint, A Visitors Guide. Columbus, OH: Blue & Gray Enterprises, 2002, 3-25.

Ankrum, Freeman. "Antietam, Maryland, Dunker Bible." *The Brethren Evangelist*, November 17, 1951, 5-6, 10-11.

———. "The Antietam Bible." *Gospel Messenger*, February 16, 1952, 10-12.

———. *Maryland and Pennsylvania Historical Sketches*. West Newton, PA: Times-Sun for the author, 1947.

———. *Sidelights on Brethren History*. Elgin, IL: Brethren Press, 1962.

"Antietam." Antietam National Battlefield, Maryland, National Park Service, U. S. Department of the Interior, GPO, Reprint 2009. (Pamphlet)

Antietam Centennial Commemorative Coin, 1962: http://americancivilwar relics.com/Civil%20War%20Antietam.htm.

Antietam Forever Stamp: http://about.usps.com/news/national-releases/2012/pr12_047.htm;

"Antietam: Shrine or Gas Station?" *Baltimore American*, September 13, 1959.

Antietam National Battlefield, 150ᵗʰ Anniversary of the Battle of Antietam, Event Program, September 14-17, 2012. 24-page document, Antietam National Battlefield Library-Archives.

Axelson, Axel. "Visiting Old Battle Fields." *Confederate Veteran*, November 1926, 418.

Bach, Jeff. *Voices of the Turtledoves: The Sacred World of Ephrata*. University Park, PA: Pennsylvania State University Press; Gottingen, Germany: Vandenhoeck & Ruprecht, 2003.

Bailey, Ronald H., and the editors of Time-Life. *The Bloodiest Day: The Battle of Antietam*. Alexandria, VA: Time-Life Books, 1984.

Barkley, Terry. "Antietam, Battle of." *The Brethren Encyclopedia*, 4 vols. Philadelphia, PA, and Oak Brook, IL: The Brethren Encyclopedia, Inc., vol. 1, 1983, 41-42.

———. *One Who Served: Brethren Elder Charles Nesselrodt of Shenandoah County, Virginia*. 3rd ed. Staunton, VA: Lot's Wife Publishing, 2004.

Battle of Antietam Centennial and Hagerstown Bicentennial: Official Program and Historical Guide, Aug. 31 Through Sept. 17, 1962. Washington County and Frederick County, MD: Antietam-South Mountain Centennial Association, Inc., 1962.

"Battle Church Restoral Set." *The Washington Post*, September 18, 1960.

Bittinger, Emmert. *Heritage and Promise: Perspectives on the Church of the Brethren.* Elgin, IL: Brethren Press, 1970.

Bowman, Carl F. *Brethren Society: The Cultural Transformation of a "Peculiar People."* Baltimore, MD: The Johns Hopkins University Press in cooperation with the Center for American Places, Harrisonburg, VA, 1995.

The Brethren Encyclopedia. 4 vols. Philadelphia, PA: The Brethren Encyclopedia, Inc., 1983-2005. "Antietam, Battle of," vol. 1, 41-42; "Church of the Brethren," vol. 1, 298-305; "Elder," vol. 1, 432; "Ministry," vol. 2, 844-845.

Carman, Ezra A., Clemens, Thomas G., ed. *The Maryland Campaign of 1862.*, 3 vols. *Antietam* vol. 2. El Dorado Hills, CA: Savas Beatie, 2012.

Clem, Richard. "Civil War Footsteps: Black Farmer Plays Key Role in Return of Dunkard Bible," *Maryland Cracker Barrel*, December/January 2004, 10, 12, 14.

———. "Travels and Travails of 'Battlefield Bible'," *The Washington Times,* June 18, 2004. *The Washington Times Online* at www.washingtontimes.com/news/2004/jun/18/20040618-080728-4573r/#ixzz2DfXk.

Clemens, Thomas G. "In Search of McClellan's Headquarters," *Civil War Times*, June 2016, 26-33.

Colby, Newton T. *The Civil War Papers of Lt. Colonel Newton T. Colby, New York Infantry.* William E. Hughes, ed. Jefferson, NC, and London: McFarland & Company, Inc., Publishers, 2003.

"Contradictions and Divided Loyalties, Slavery on the Antietam Battleground: A Companion Guide to the Auto Tour for School Groups": www.nps.gov/anti/learn/education/upload/Contradictions-and-Divided-Loyalties.pdf.

Cooper, H. Austin. "Antietam Battlefield Landmark to be Reconstructed." From *Antietam Dunkard Church* (his unpublished book), New Windsor, MD. Rev. H. Austin Cooper Collection, Brethren Historical Library and Archives, Church of the Brethren General Offices, Elgin, IL.

———. *Antietam Dunkard Church* (unpublished book). Austin Cooper Collection, BHLA, Elgin, IL.

———. "A Brief Sketch of the Development of the Reconstruction Project, 1960-1962," August 31, 1962, New Windsor, MD. In "Antietam Battlefield Dunker Church Rededication, September 2, 1962" (Booklet). Austin Cooper Collection, BHLA, Elgin, IL.

———. "Upon This Rock—Build," in *Antietam Dunkard Church* (unpublished) . Austin Cooper Collection, BHLA, Elgin, IL.

Cooper, H. Austin and Arthur Scrogum. "The Dunker Church and the Church of the Brethren." The Middle Maryland District and the General Brotherhood Board of the Church of the Brethren, undated. (Pamphlet)

Cowper, William. Hymn: "God Moves in Mysterious Ways." 1774.

Cox, Jacob D. *Military Reminiscences of the Civil War.* New York: C. Scribner's Sons, 1900.

The Dedication of the Reconstructed Dunker Church, September, 2, 1962, 1:30 p.m., Antietam National Battlefield Site, Sharpsburg, Maryland. Rededication program on file in Antietam National Battlefield Library-Archives.

Delaplaine, Edward S. *Lincoln's Companions on the Trip to Antietam.* Harrogate, TN: Lincoln Memorial University Press, 1954.

Douglas, Henry Kyd and Fletcher M. Green. *I Rode With Stonewall.* Chapel Hill: University of North Carolina Press, 1940, 1961.

Doyle, Vernell and Tim Doyle. *Sharpsburg.* Charleston, SC: Arcadia Publishing, 2009.

"The Dunkard Church." National Park Service: Antietam National Battlefield, Maryland. Revised 1965. (Pamphlet)

"The Dunker Church." Antietam National Battlefield Site, U. S. Department of the Interior, National Park Service, undated, c. 1962. (Booklet)

"The Dunker Church: A Battlefield Shrine." Undated and unnumbered four-page teaching tool with questions for students.

"Dunker Church Rededicated Despite Inclement Weather." Hagerstown, MD: *The Daily Mail*, September 14, 1962.

"Eisenhower Signs Antietam Park Bill." *The Washington Post*, November 23, 1960.

Ernst, Kathleen. *Too Afraid to Cry: Maryland Civilians in the Antietam Campaign.* Mechanicsburg, PA: Stackpole Press, 1999.

"First Visitor to 'New' Dunker Church." Hagerstown, MD: *The Morning Herald*, July 12, 1962.

40th Annual Dunker Church Worship Service, September 19, 2010, Antietam National Battlefield, Sharpsburg, Maryland, Sponsored by Churches of the Brethren in Maryland and West Virginia, unnumbered pages. (Booklet)

Frassanito, William A. *Antietam: The Photographic Legacy of America's Bloodiest Day.* New York: Scribner, 1978.

Gallagher, Gary W. *The Antietam Campaign.* Chapel Hill, NC: University of North Carolina Press, 1999.

Gordon, Ronald J. "Little Dunker Church: A Silent Witness for Peace." Church of the Brethren Network, August 1988, last updated March 2013, www.cob-net.org/antietam/.

———. "Peace is Witnessed" from "Little Dunker Church: A Silent Witness for Peace." Church of the Brethren Network, August 1988, last updated March 2013, www.cob-net.org/antietam/.

Hagerstown, Maryland: http://www.hagerstownmd.org/.

Harman, Charles William. "Restoration of Old Dunkard Church Planned at Antietam." Hagerstown, MD: *The Morning Herald*, March 3, 1937.

Harsh, Joseph. *Taken at the Flood: Robert E. Lee and Confederate Strategy in the Maryland Campaign of 1862.* Kent, OH: Kent State University, 1999.

Henry, Jerry Maurice. *History of the Church of the Brethren in Maryland.* Elgin, IL: Brethren Publishing House, 1936.

Hicks, E. Russell. "The Church on the Battlefield." Part One. Church of the Brethren *Gospel Messenger*, February 2, 1952, 9.

——. "The Church on the Battlefield." Part Two. Church of the Brethren *Gospel Messenger* February 9, 1952, 14.

Hillinger, Charles. Charles Hillinger's America. "Marking 125th Anniversary of Antietam Battle." *Los Angeles Times*, September 20, 1987, http://articles.latimes.com/1987-09-20/news/vw-9238_1_125th-anniversary/2.

Kalasky, Robert J. *Shadows of Antietam*. Kent, OH: The Kent State University Press, 2012.

Krensky, Stephen. *Clara Barton.* New York, NY: DK Publishing, 2011.

Longenecker, Stephen L. *Gettysburg Religion: Refinement, Diversity, and Race in the Antebellum and Civil War Border North.* New York: Fordham University Press, 2014.

Luvass, Jay and Harold W. Nelson. *Guide to the Battle of Antietam, the Maryland Campaign of 1862.* Lawrence, KS: University Press of Kansas, 1996.

"The Manor Church of the Brethren, Mother of the Dunkard Church of Antietam Battlefield." A two-page unsigned document which was apparently produced by the Manor Church of the Brethren, Tilghmanton, MD.

McPherson, James M. *Crossroads of Freedom: Antietam.* New York: Oxford University Press, 2002.

Mullikin, James C. "Civil War Centennial Group Lauded For Plan to Rebuild Antietam Church." *Baltimore American*, May 1, 1960.

Murfin, James V. *The Gleam of Bayonets: The Battle of Antietam and the Maryland Campaign of 1862.* New York: T. Yoseloff, 1965.

"New 'Keys' Are Designed For City: Wood from Historical Dunker Church, Hager Home to Be Used." Possibly in the Hagerstown, MD, *Morning Herald*, date unknown.

Noyes, George F. *The Bivouac and the Battlefield; or, Campaign Sketches in Virginia and Maryland.* New York: Harper and Brothers, 1863.

125th Anniversary, Battle of Antietam Program of Events, September 12-27, 1987, unpaged. Antietam National Battlefield Library-Archives.

Otto, Ruth. "What I Remember About Dunker Church." Sharpsburg, MD, February 6, 1962, five unnumbered pages. Austin Cooper Collection, BHLA, Elgin, IL.

Paine, Albert B. *Mark Twain: A Biography.* vol. 2. New York & London: Harper & Brothers, 1912.

Palfrey, Francis. *The Antietam and Fredericksburg.* New York: C. Scribner's Sons, 1882.

Picerno, Nicholas P. Military service records of Nathan F. and James F. Dykeman, and Calvin Blanchard, Union Database, Bridgewater, Virginia.

Platou, Arnold S. *After the Dunker Church...One Hundred Years of Faithful Service, 1899-1999.* Sharpsburg Church of the Brethren. Sharpsburg, MD: Unknown publisher, 1999.

Poling, Newton L. "The Dunkers: Their Customs and Life Style in the Antietam Valley." A paper delivered by Rev. Poling at the 1992 Antietam Volunteer Seminar in Hagerstown, MD, March 21, 1992.

Priest, John M. *Antietam: The Soldiers' Battle.* Shippensburg, PA: White Mane Publishing Company, 1989.

Program for the Eighteen-Day Centennial Commemoration of the Battle of Antietam and Hagerstown, Md., Bicentennial, August 31-September 17, 1962. Blue insert to *Battle of Antietam Centennial and Hagerstown Bicentennial Official Program and Historical Guide, Aug. 31 Through Sept. 17, 1962.*

Ramirez, Frank. "Antietam Meetinghouse: Old Bibles and Radical Compassion." Church of the Brethren *Messenger*, November 2010, 8-11.

Reardon, Carol and Tom Vossler. *A Field Guide to Antietam: Experiencing the Battlefield Through Its History, Places, and People.* Chapel Hill, NC: The University of North Carolina Press, 2016.

"Reconstructed Dunker Church at Antietam Open to Public." Hagerstown, MD: *The Daily Mail*, July 7, 1962.

Reilly, Oliver T. *The Battlefield of Antietam.* Sharpsburg, MD: O. T. Reilly, 1906.

Robertson, James I., Jr. *Stonewall Jackson: The Man, The Soldier, The Legend.* New York: Macmillan Publishing USA; London: Prentice Hall International, 1997.

Rosenberger, Mary Sue. "Conversation at Antietam." Church of the Brethren *Messenger*, November 2010, 9.

Rubin, Mary H. *Hagerstown.* Charleston, SC: Arcadia Publishing, 2001.

Rupel, Esther Fern. *Brethren Dress: A Testimony to Faith.* Philadelphia, PA: The Brethren Encyclopedia, 1994.

Sachse, Julius F. *German Sectarians of Pennsylvania.* vol. 1, 1708-1742. Philadelphia, PA: For the author by P. C. Stockhausen, 1899-1900.

Scheppard, Carol A. and Samuel Sarpiya and Dale E. Minnich. "When Lamentations Are Not Enough: A Statement for the Church of the Brethren." *Newsline*, Church of the Brethren online, July 12, 2016, www.brethren.org/news/2016/church-leaders-call-brethren-to-be-refuge-during-violence.html.

Schildt, John W. *Drums Along the Antietam.* Parsons, WV: McClain Printing Company, 1972.

———. *Four Days in October.* Chewsville, MD: John W. Schildt, 1978, 1982.

Schmidt, Alann. "Antietam's Dunker Church: Beacon of Peace." *Brethren Life & Thought*, fall 2012, 1-14.

——. "Beacon of Peace: Antietam's Dunker Church." *Antietam Journal*, January 8, 2013, http://antietamjournal.blogspot.com/2013/02/beacon-of-peace-antietams-dunker-church.html.

——. Draft, *Historic American Buildings Survey, Dunker Church, Antietam National Battlefield,* unpaged.

Seachrist, Denise A. *Snow Hill: In the Shadows of the Ephrata Cloister*. Kent, OH: Kent State University Press, 2010.

Sears, Stephen W. *George B. McClellan: The Young Napoleon*. New York: Ticknor & Fields, 1988.

——. *Landscape Turned Red: The Battle of Antietam*. New Haven, CT: Ticknor & Fields, 1983.

Sharpsburg, Maryland: http://sharpsburgmd.com/.

"State and Nation Have Helped Veterans Adorn Picturesque Antietam Battlefield." *The Washington Post*, September 15, 1907, M8.

Stepp, John W. "Task Force of House Weighs Antietam Field." Washington, D.C.: *Evening Star*, April 11, 1959.

Sullivan, Lori Lynn. "A Battle, a Brown Bundle & a Black Farmer," at https://lorilynnsullivan.com/tag/dunkard-bible/.

"Tawes Offers Help For '62 Civil War Centennial Here." Hagerstown, MD: *The Daily Mail*, June 10, 1959.

Thomasson, Kermon. "Mark Twain and His Dunker Friend." Church of the Brethren *Messenger,* October 1985, 19, 21.

Thoreau, Henry David and Stephen Fender. *Walden*. Oxford & New York: Oxford University Press, 2008.

Tolson's Chapel, Sharpsburg, MD: http://www.tolsonschapel.org/.

Trail, Susan W. *Remembering Antietam: Commemoration and Preservation of a Civil War Battlefield*. Ph. D. dissertation. College Park, MD: University of Maryland, 2005.

Walker, Kevin M. and K. C. Kirkman. *Antietam Farmsteads: A Guide to the Battlefield Landscape.* Sharpsburg, MD: Western Maryland Interpretive Association, 2010.

Washington County, Maryland: http://washco-md.net/.

Wert, Jeffry. *The Sword of Lincoln: The Army of the Potomac*. New York: Simon & Schuster, 2005.

Williams, Thomas J. C. *A History of Washington County, Maryland*. Baltimore, MD: Regional Publishing Company, 1968.

Wisbey, Herbert A., Jr. "John T. Lewis, Mark Twain's Friend in Elmira." Elmira, NY: *Mark Twain Society Bulletin*, January 1984, 4.

Index

Acknowledgments

Alann Schmidt

I would like to first and foremost thank the Lord for blessing me with so many wonderful opportunities throughout my life, whatever my situation. Phil. 4:8-9.

I would most like to thank my co-author, Terry Barkley, for making this book happen. Unfortunately my ranger career was cut short by a serious illness in 2015, and I came to accept that the Dunker Church research I had been working on was a missed opportunity—and then Terry contacted me! He took it over and made it so much more than I could have done on my own.

I would also like to thank: The Church of the Brethren community who welcomed me, notably Frank Ramirez, Jeff Bach, Nick Picerno, Steve Longenecker, and Paul Roth; my National Park Service family, notably friends Brian Baracz, John Hoptak, Dan Vermilya, Keith Snyder, and Ted Alexander; the NPS/ Sharpsburg/Civil War community who supported me and/or shared information, notably Ike Mumma, Betty Otto-Kretzer, Earl Roulette, Philip Roulette, Susan Trail, Jane Custer, Keven Walker, Craig Cartwright, Ed Wenschhof, Christie Stanczak, Jim Buchanan, Tom Clemens, Mike Gamble, Joe Calzarette, Mannie Gentile, Steve Recker, Matt Borders, and Vance and Elisabeth Creech, among others.

A special thank you is due Shippensburg University professor Steve Burg for inspiring me to pursue a history career in the first place.

Finally, I owe a big thank you to my family for their tremendous love and support, especially my wife Tracy and my parents, Paul & Susie Schmidt.

Terry Barkley

First and foremost, I thank Alann Schmidt for allowing me to collaborate with him in completing this book. Alann had been working diligently on his book hoping to have it completed and released in time for the Sesquicentennial of the Battle of Antietam on September 17, 2012. Life, however, intervened, and medical complications eventually led to his retirement from the National Park Service. The book project on the Dunker Church faded away as Alann struggled with the long-term debilitating effects of Lyme disease.

Throughout Alann's ordeal, his wife, Tracy, has been a godsend and a helpmate. Their lives are now moving in a new direction, towards the ordained ministry of the Church of God.

A special thank you to Ted Alexander, retired historian at Antietam National Battlefield, for his wonderful Foreword and the detailed appendix about the fighting around the Dunker Church. Ted read this manuscript for all things Antietam-related, and Brethren historian Dr. Jeff Bach, director of the Young Center for Anabaptist and Pietist Studies at Elizabethtown College in Pennsylvania, a Brethren-related college, for all things Brethren-related.

I dedicated part of this book to Rev. H. Austin Cooper, Church of the Brethren minister and historian. Austin was on the front lines of the fight to rebuild the church on its original site. He was working on a book entitled *Antietam Dunkard Church*, but was unable to finish it; he did publish several other church histories. Austin, pastor of the Sharpsburg Church of the Brethren in the 1940s, passed in 1999.

Larry and Alice Cooper of Landenberg, Pa., donated Rev. Cooper's papers to the Brethren Historical Library and Archives (BHLA) in Elgin, Ill., in 2011, when I was its director. The papers had been picked over by family and friends before being stored in a shed for years, but much of Austin's work on the Dunker Church remained, and I have used it liberally to complete this book. Bill Kostlevy, the present director of the BHLA, and Fred Miller, Bill's archival assistant, were helpful in fulfilling my several requests for materials for the book.

I would also like to thank:

Dr. Emmert Bittinger, a retired professor of sociology at Bridgewater College in Virginia with a deep interest in the Dunker Church who served as a pastor of the Sharpsburg Church of the Brethren in the 1950s. I visited with Emmert and his wife Esther in their home at the Bridgewater Retirement Community in August 2016.

Betty J. Otto, park historian in the late 70s and early 80s when I was researching the church, gave me a splendid tour of Brethren sites around Sharpsburg. She was married to the late Page T. (Ted) Otto. Remarried, she is now Betty Otto-Kretzer.

Stephanie Gray of Antietam National Battlefield's Museum and Library Services allowed me to research the 125th and 150th anniversaries of the battle.

Historian Edie Wallace gave me, Alann, Ted Alexander, and Jeff Bach a personal tour of Tolson's Chapel, an historic African-American church (1866-1998) in Sharpsburg, and clarified questions about African-American history in the area.

Cartographer Steven A. Stanley of Gettysburg, Pa., drafted the fine maps.

Some of the research and nearly all of the actual writing for this book was done in the fine academic libraries at Washington & Lee University and Virginia Military Institute in Lexington. The staffs at both institutions were helpful and friendly.

I must also thank Gary Langley, Kevin McCann, and Seth McCormick-Goodhart for their vital contributions.

There are some words and phrases used in this book that denote gender and which may be deemed sexist by some Brethren women. This terminology was in use during the day when the eldership (abolished in 1967 in the Church of the Brethren) provided male-dominated leadership to the "Brotherhood." Things are changing or have changed in the church today, and female leadership is beginning to dominate at both the congregational, district, and national/international levels. The contributions of the "women's fellowship" at the congregational level have been myriad throughout the history of the Brethren.

Alann and I would both like to thank our publisher, Savas Beatie, and everyone there for all the assistance in preparing this manuscript for publication.

Finally, I want to thank my sister, Betty J. Barkley-Fawley, for her love and support.

Alann Schmidt spent fifteen years as a park ranger at Antietam National Battlefield. He presented hundreds of programs on the Dunker Church to park visitors, Civil War seminars, community groups, churches, and for Brethren Heritage tours.

He earned degrees from the University of Pittsburgh, Shippensburg University, Shepherd University, and the Pittsburgh Institute of Mortuary Science. While illness forced Alann into early retirement, he still serves as a pastor for the Churches of God and helps foster pets for rescue groups. He and his wife Tracy (and their many cats) live on their family farm near Fort Littleton, Pennsylvania.

About the Authors

Terry Barkley served as archivist and museum curator at Bridgewater College in Virginia, a Brethren-related institution, and holds degrees and a graduate certificate from the University of North Alabama, The Citadel, University of Alabama, and Harvard University. He retired in 2012 as director of the Brethren Historical Library and Archives (BHLA) at the Church of the Brethren General Offices in Elgin, Illinois. That same year (2012), he delivered the 150th (sesquicentennial) anniversary commemorative lecture on the Dunker Church of Antietam Battlefield at the Annual Conference of the Church of the Brethren in St. Louis. Terry has also lectured in the Dunker Church at Antietam.

An independent scholar and musician, Terry lives in Lexington, Virginia. This is his fourth book.